RODALE'S
GARDEN-FRESH COOKING

Hundreds of ways to cook, serve, and store your favorite fresh vegetables and fruits

Produced by the Food Center and the Photography Department of Rodale Press

Text and recipes by Judith Benn Hurley

Rodale Press, Emmaus, Pennsylvania

To my sweetheart, Pat Hurley

Book design and layout by Glen Burris, Linda Jacopetti, and Jerry O'Brien

Photographers: John P. Hamel, Carl Doney, Sally Shenk Ullman, Mitchell T.
Mandel, Alison Miksch, Christie C. Tito, and Angelo M. Caggiano

Stylists: Kay Seng Lichthardt, Laura Hendry Reifsnyder, Barbara Fritz,
Virginia Barz, and Marianne G. Laubbach

Library of Congress Cataloging-in-Publication Data

Hurley, Judith Benn.
    Rodale's garden-fresh cooking.

    Includes index.
    1. Cookery (Vegetables)   2. Cookery (Fruit)
I. Title
TX801.H87   1987   641.6′5   86–33880
ISBN   0–87857–694–0   hardcover
ISBN   0–87857–695–9   paperback

2 4 6 8 10 9 7 5 3 1   hardcover
2 4 6 8 10 9 7 5 3 1   paperback

Contents

Acknowledgments

Are you the type of person who leaves a movie before the credits are over? Of course not, that would be rude. And besides, you'd miss knowing about all the work that went into the makings. Well, the same thing goes for books. Many fine people contributed to *Rodale's Garden-Fresh Cooking,* so read this page.

Special thanks to:

Nancy J. Zelko, JoAnn Brader, and Beth Pianucci for recipe development.

JoAnn Brader, Natalie Updegrove, Beth Pianucci, and Nancy J. Zelko for recipe testing.

Nancy J. Zelko and Sarah Leonard for research.

Marilee Stahler for finding fresh strawberries in January, baby beets in February, and a year-round supply of fresh herbs.

The Allentown Farmer's Market and Shop Rite, Allentown, Pennsylvania; the Rodale Research Center; Dan Schantz Farm Market, Emmaus, Pennsylvania; Wilcox Roadside Market, Boyertown, Pennsylvania; Ulrich's Produce, Reading, Pennsylvania; Stauffer's Seafood at the Shillington Farmer's Market and Pathmark, Shillington, Pennsylvania; and Balducci's, New York, for special orders and special attention.

Tom Gettings, Director of Rodale's Photography Department, and Tom Ney, Director of Rodale's Food Center, for planting the seeds for this book.

The staff of *Rodale's Organic Gardening* magazine, especially Susan Milius, Rudy Keller, Ellen Cohen, David Riggle, Vicki Mattern, and Marie Scott, for their gardening expertise.

Julie Mayers for proofreading with her discriminating eye.

Sarah Leonard for her organizational and word-processing skills.

Hitchcock Cleaning and Emily Folland for sparkling kitchens.

Dyla, Bill, Antoinette, Bruce, Gail, Tom, Hayes, Megan, Simon, and Vanessa for tasting, tasting, and retasting.

It has been an exceptional privilege to work with three super editors. Special thanks to Camille Bucci for her knowledge of food and recipes, to Anne Halpin for her good taste and support, and to Charlie Gerras for his encouragement and for giving me the opportunity to write this book.

Introduction

Rodale's Garden-Fresh Cooking is the fantasy-come-true of a group of food lovers—a chef, a team of photographers, a food writer, food stylists, garden editors, and food editors—to present truly exciting and new ideas for using popular vegetables and fruits. By ideas, we mean not just the usual recipes for how to make a tomato sauce, but instead a slew of delightful options for what to do when you've got a million tomatoes in the kitchen and more on the way!

Recipes that maintain the produce in a close-to-fresh state, that is the ideal we pursue. In this book you won't find unidentified mush. Consider, for instance, Grilled Marinated Tomatoes, freshly picked then sizzled on the grill until their skins burnish and their flesh is silken. Then they're tossed with fresh basil, garlic, and a splash of fruity olive oil and served with pasta or crusty bread.

We have focused on America's twelve most popular garden vegetables and six favorite homegrown fruits. You can use this book as a market guide or as a garden manual. For example, the harvest information for each vegetable and fruit will tell gardeners when to pluck and non-gardeners when to buy. The ripening and storage information, the culinary tips and variety comparisons, are valuable to any cook—gardener or not.

Flip through the pages for a hint of what's to come: Peppers with Saffron and Pan-Fried Noodles, Peach-Glazed Spareribs, Corn and Spinach Strudel, Carrot Coins with Chicken and Feta. The recipes, though imaginative, are comfortable and easy to prepare. Many require just a few ingredients and can be prepared using familiar cooking techniques.

What you may not notice at first is that the recipes are healthful. That doesn't mean brown, boring, and devoid of flavor and texture. To us, healthful food is low in fat, low in calories, contains no added salt and no refined sugar, *and* it's appetizing. Think of plump steamed shrimp with strawberries and snow peas drizzled with raspberry vinaigrette, or julienne of pears baked with a slab of tasty swordfish. The secret of these recipes is in the art of selecting flavor combinations to satisfy the senses.

Creating this book has been for me a culinary adventure filled with discovery and fun. I hope that it will be the same for everybody who uses it.

Judith Hurley
Reading, Pennsylvania
1987

CHAPTER 1

GREEN BEANS

If you have the rare opportunity to sample beans just when the pods have formed, don't pass it up. Instead, steam the tiny, tender vegetables for about a minute. Then pat them dry and toss with a splash of melted sweet butter and tarragon or fruity olive oil and thyme. Even if you can't have baby beans, try for the small and slender ones. Why eat big tough beans you have to cook for hours?

Vinegar-based marinades and lemon dressings make beans sparkle, as do mushrooms, nuts, tomatoes, onions, corn, chives, chervil, savory, dill, and shallots.

INTO THE BASKET

- Beans are ready to pick about a week after blossoms appear. The beans should be no fatter than a pencil; they should "snap" when broken, and seeds should be barely visible.
- When harvesting, use your thumbnail and index finger to pinch each bean gently at the stem. Never tug on the bean because it could damage the plant.
- If you harvest beans before the seeds become really visible, more blossoms will form and that means a bigger harvest.
- If you let the beans "go by" and the seeds grow to full size, many varieties can be harvested prior to frost and eaten as shell beans.

INDOOR STORAGE

- To keep beans for three or four days, rinse them off but don't dry them. This will help retain moisture. Then put the beans in a plastic bag in which you have poked a few holes, and refrigerate. You can also blanch the beans for a minute or two, just until they become bright green. Then store them like raw beans, for about a week.
- If you've let your beans mature and have harvested shell beans, they'll keep for about two weeks in a sealed plastic bag. They freeze well, too.

CULINARY TECHNIQUES

Weights and Measures

1 pound untrimmed whole beans
> = 4 cups trimmed halved beans
> = 4 cups trimmed and diagonally sliced (1-inch pieces) beans
> = 4 cups trimmed and chopped beans
> = 3½ cups trimmed and finely diced beans

1 pound trimmed steamed beans
> = 2 cups coarse puree

1 pound trimmed steamed beans pureed with ¼ cup stock
> = 2½ cups fine puree

The French Cut

This is a thin, vertical cut, easily made with a sharp 8- or 10-inch knife. A long-bladed kitchen shears works well, too.

The Chinese Cut

For visual interest and flavor, the Chinese often cut their beans on a diagonal.

Avoiding Squeakers

To some people, the only thing worse than fingernails on a blackboard is biting into a squeaky green bean. This can be avoided by steaming the beans for four or five minutes before adding to salads or stir fries.

OK, NEXT YEAR

- Although most varieties need warm soil to thrive, Provider, Royal Burgundy, Astro, and Lancer are cold tolerant for short-season growing.
- Bush varieties offer early planting and are less sensitive to drought and heat than pole beans. Some varieties to try are Tendercrop, Top Crop, Green Ruler, Contender, Provider, Spartan Arrow, Bush Romano (broad), and Jumbo (broad).
- Pole varieties can be bigger producers than bush varieties. Try Kentucky Wonder, Italian Romano (broad), Blue Lake, and Scarlet Runner (known for its decorative scarlet flowers).
- Wax varieties are easy to pick because they're easy to see. Varieties include Cherokee, Sungold, Goldcrop, Moongold, Keygold, Beurre de Rocquencourt, Easter Butterwax, and Kinghorn Special.
- Varieties that freeze well include Blue Lake, Slenderwhite, Romano, Tendercrop, Tenderette, and Topcrop.
- Interplanting nasturtium, garlic, or potatoes may help repel the Mexican bean beetle. Regal and Goldcrop Yellow are two varieties that are somewhat resistant to the pest.
- Dade is a pole variety that produces well in hot climates.
- Royalty, Blue Coco, Royal Burgundy, and Royal Burgundy Bush are purple-podded beans that turn green when cooked. They are also somewhat resistant to the Mexican bean beetle.
- Bush Blue Lake 274, Bush Blue Lake 47, and State Half Runner have good resistance to bean yellow mosaic virus (BYMV).

Tiny Crepes
with Green Beans and Garlic

makes about 16 appetizers

Crepes:
½ cup whole wheat flour
 1 cup unbleached white flour
 3 eggs, room temperature
¾ cup water
½ cup milk
 2 tablespoons butter, melted
¼ cup minced, cooked green beans
⅛ teaspoon minced fresh thyme or pinch of dried thyme
　 corn oil

Filling:
 2 teaspoons corn oil
½ cup finely chopped green beans
 1 small clove garlic, minced
 3 ounces cream cheese or yogurt cheese, room temperature
　 dash of ground nutmeg

Sauce:
½ cup plain yogurt
 1 teaspoon Dijon mustard

　　To prepare the crepes: In a blender or food processor, combine whole wheat flour and white flour, eggs, water, milk, and butter. Blend until smooth, pausing to scrape down sides of container with a spatula. Pour into a bowl. Stir in beans and thyme. Let batter stand for 1 hour.

　　Brush a small nonstick skillet with corn oil. Heat over medium-high heat until very hot (a drop of water should sizzle). Pour in 2 teaspoons of batter, quickly spread with a spatula to a 2½-inch round, and cook until golden on bottom and dry on top. Turn over and cook other side until dry. Remove and let cool. Repeat with remaining batter. Batter should be the consistency of light cream. Thin with water if it thickens while standing. Crepes may be prepared 1 day ahead of time, covered, and refrigerated.

　　To prepare the filling: Heat oil in a medium-size nonstick skillet. Add chopped beans and garlic and cook until beans are tender, about 5 minutes, stirring occasionally. Cool. In a small bowl, combine bean mixture with cream cheese and nutmeg.

　　Spread ½ teaspoon of filling on each crepe. Roll up and place in a serving dish.

　　To prepare the sauce: Mix yogurt and mustard together in a small bowl. Serve crepes with sauce on the side.

Marinated Green Beans and Favas

4 to 6 servings

  1 teaspoon minced garlic
¼ teaspoon dry mustard
    freshly ground black pepper to taste
  2 tablespoons balsamic or red wine vinegar
  3 tablespoons olive oil
  2 tablespoons chopped fresh basil
1½ cups cooked fava beans, shelled and split
  1 pound green beans, cut into 1-inch pieces
  2 tablespoons finely chopped red onions

     In a small bowl, whisk together garlic, mustard, pepper, and vinegar. Slowly whisk in oil, continuing to whisk until thoroughly emulsified. Stir in basil.

     In a small bowl, toss fava beans with half of the dressing. Cover and let marinate for 1 hour.

     Steam green beans until tender. Drain; pat dry. Toss with remaining dressing.

     Arrange fava beans in center of serving dish. Spoon green beans around favas. Sprinkle with red onions and serve with crusty bread or in lettuce cups on chilled plates.

Green Beans Caught in a Net

4 to 6 servings

½ pound green beans, trimmed
1 tablespoon dried, chopped lemongrass*
3 fresh basil leaves
2 small slices ginger root
2 cloves garlic, crushed
3 tablespoons rice vinegar
1 teaspoon sesame oil
2 eggs, room temperature, beaten

Steam beans for about 5 minutes. While beans are still warm, toss with lemongrass, basil, ginger, garlic, vinegar, and oil in a medium-size bowl and let marinate for at least 1 hour.

To make the nets, heat a nonstick skillet over medium heat and give eggs a final swirl to make sure they're combined. Then dip 4 fingertips of one hand into eggs and immediately glide your fingertips over surface of skillet, trailing threads as you go. Get as close to surface of skillet as you can without burning your fingers. Quickly dip same fingers back in egg and make another set of 4 threads, crosswise over the first. Continue by making 2 more sets of diagonal threads. Let net cook until it has set, then remove it gently with a spatula. Continue making nets until there is no more egg.

To assemble, grab 3 beans, shake off their marinade, set them on edge of a net, and roll.

*Lemongrass is available at specialty food stores and health food stores.

Green Beans with Tuna

4 servings

4 cups cut green beans (1-inch pieces)
1 can (7 ounces) solid-white, water-packed tuna, drained
2 tablespoons finely chopped scallions
2 tablespoons finely chopped fresh Italian parsley
1 teaspoon minced fresh basil or ½ teaspoon dried basil
3 tablespoons olive oil, divided
1 tablespoon lemon juice
1 clove garlic, minced
  freshly ground black pepper to taste
1 ripe tomato, quartered, for garnish
  sieved hard-cooked egg for garnish

Steam green beans until just tender.

In a small bowl, combine tuna, scallions, parsley, and basil.

Whisk together 2 tablespoons of the oil, lemon juice, garlic, and pepper. Pour over tuna. Mix gently.

Toss remaining oil with beans. Arrange on a serving dish. Mound tuna mixture in center and garnish with tomato and egg.

Green Bean Soup with Lentils and Chick-peas

4 to 6 servings

1 tablespoon vegetable oil
½ cup minced celery
½ cup minced onions
½ cup minced carrots
1 clove garlic, minced
    bouquet garni—3 sprigs parsley, 3 sprigs chervil
        (or 1 teaspoon dried chervil), 3 sprigs thyme (or
        ½ teaspoon dried thyme), and 2 bay leaves, gathered
        together in a piece of cheesecloth and tied with string
6 cups vegetable stock
½ cup dried lentils, picked over and rinsed
2 cups cut green beans (1-inch pieces)
1 cup cooked chick-peas (drain and rinse, if canned)
2 medium-size tomatoes, peeled, seeded, and chopped
    minced fresh parsley for garnish

Heat oil in a 4-quart saucepan over medium-low heat. Add celery, onions, carrots, and garlic, and cook until vegetables are soft, about 5 minutes. Add bouquet garni, stock, and lentils. Bring to a boil. Reduce heat, cover, and simmer about 45 minutes, or until lentils are tender.

Add green beans, chick-peas, and tomatoes, and cook 10 to 15 minutes longer, or until green beans are tender. Remove bouquet garni and serve garnished with parsley.

Fragrant Haddock with Vegetables

4 servings

1 pound green beans, cut into 1-inch pieces
1 pound haddock fillets, cut into serving pieces
¼ cup whole wheat flour
3 tablespoons olive oil
⅓ cup chopped red onions
⅓ cup chopped celery
1 small green pepper, seeded and cut into ½-inch squares
3 strips (2 × 1 inch) orange peel
¼ teaspoon fennel seeds, lightly crushed
1 sprig thyme or ½ teaspoon dried thyme
1 bay leaf
1 cup chicken or fish stock
2 plum tomatoes, peeled, seeded, and chopped
   generous pinch of crushed saffron, dissolved in
        1 tablespoon water
2 tablespoons apple cider vinegar

Steam beans until just tender.

Dust haddock with flour, shaking off excess. Place in a baking dish. Bake at 425°F until fish flakes easily. Keep warm in a very low oven.

In a medium-size skillet, heat oil over medium-low heat. Add onions, celery, and pepper, and cook for 10 minutes, or until vegetables are soft. Add orange peel, fennel seeds, thyme, and bay leaf, and cook, stirring constantly, for 30 seconds. Add stock and tomatoes, bring to a boil, and boil until liquid is reduced by one-third. Remove bay leaf. Add saffron with water, beans, and vinegar, and bring just to a boil. Pour sauce over fish and serve.

Butterflies and Beans

4 servings

¾ pound green beans, cut into ½-inch pieces
½ cup fresh basil leaves
½ cup fresh parsley leaves
 1 clove garlic, coarsely chopped
 1 tablespoon chopped fresh chives
⅛ teaspoon crushed dried rosemary
⅓ cup grated Parmesan cheese
 3 tablespoons olive oil
 2 tablespoons chicken stock
 2 fresh spinach leaves
¾ pound farfalle pasta (butterflies), cooked

Steam beans until tender.

In a food processor or blender, combine basil, parsley, garlic, chives, rosemary, and cheese. Process until chopped. Add oil, stock, and spinach, and process until smooth.

In a warm serving bowl, combine beans and pasta. Add sauce and toss gently. Serve immediately.

Medallions of Chicken with Green Beans

4 servings

2 tablespoons vegetable oil, divided
4 scallions (white part only), sliced lengthwise
1 pound green beans, trimmed
　freshly ground black pepper to taste
4 shallots, minced
1 cup chicken stock
3 tablespoons slivered almonds, lightly toasted and ground
2 tablespoons half-and-half
2 teaspoons Dijon mustard
1 teaspoon minced fresh tarragon or ½ teaspoon dried tarragon
4 boneless chicken breast halves (about 1½ pounds),
　　　　each sliced diagonally into 5 pieces and pounded to a
　　　　¼-inch thickness

Heat 1 tablespoon of the oil in a medium-size skillet. Add scallions and beans, cover, and cook over medium-low heat, stirring occasionally, for 5 minutes. Remove from heat and season with pepper. Set aside.

In a small saucepan, heat remaining oil over medium-low heat. Add shallots and cook until tender, about 4 minutes. Add stock, bring to a boil, and boil briskly until reduced by half. Stir in almonds, half-and-half, mustard, and tarragon. Set aside to cool.

Cut 4 large, heart-shaped pieces of parchment paper or aluminum foil. Place one-quarter of the bean mixture on each piece of paper. Place 5 slices of chicken on top of each mound of green beans. Spread sauce over chicken. Fold up paper to enclose chicken and beans and place bundles on a baking sheet. Bake in a preheated 425°F oven for 20 minutes. Transfer bundles to serving dishes and cut open to serve.

The Leather Look

After harvesting, beans can be strung on long pieces of thread and hung, from the middle, in an airy place to dry. After they have dried, they look like leather trousers (the traditional name for them is leather britches), and they can be cooked in soups, stews, and ragouts until tender.

Green Beans with Peanuts and Chilies

4 servings

1 pound green beans, trimmed
2 tablespoons peanut oil
2 cloves garlic, slightly crushed
2 (2-inch) dried hot chili peppers
2 tablespoons raw blanched peanuts
1 teaspoon chili oil

Place beans in a strainer. Pour boiling water over them for 5 seconds. Drain well. Pat very dry. Set aside.

Heat a wok or large skillet over high heat until very hot, about 30 seconds. Pour in peanut oil and heat for 20 seconds. Add garlic and chili peppers, and stir-fry for 10 seconds (do not let garlic burn). Add beans and peanuts and stir-fry for 30 seconds. Remove from heat. Toss with chili oil. Serve immediately.

Green Beans
in Brown Butter with Thyme

4 servings

¾ pound green beans, trimmed
1½ tablespoons butter
  5 sprigs thyme

Steam beans until just tender.

In a heavy skillet, melt butter over very low heat until hazelnut brown. Add thyme and beans. Toss together for 30 seconds or until heated through.

Baby Bean Timbales with Dill

makes 4 timbales

½ pound green beans, trimmed
 1 tablespoon butter
 1 tablespoon whole wheat flour
 1 cup milk
 1 teaspoon Dijon mustard
¼ teaspoon dried dillweed
 2 eggs
   grated Parmesan cheese to sprinkle

Steam beans until tender and puree.

Preheat oven to 400°F. Pour about an inch of water into a baking pan and set it in oven to heat.

Meanwhile, melt butter in a medium-size saucepan and whisk in flour to form a paste. Add milk and continue to whisk until sauce thickens. Add mustard, dillweed, and eggs, puree, and combine well.

Pour mixture into 4 6-ounce custard cups that have been sprayed with vegetable spray. Carefully set filled cups in pan of water and bake for about 20 minutes.

To unmold, gently run a knife between timbale and its cup, and turn upside-down onto a plate. Serve warm with grated cheese.

Note: If you don't have custard cups, use coffee cups or tiny molds.

CHAPTER 2

BEETS

The sweet, earthy flavor and hardy texture that characterize the best beets can be guaranteed by timely harvest, proper storage, and imaginative culinary techniques.

Once best known in the sweet-and-sour preparation called Harvard, beets are showing up in all sorts of combinations. Their flavor blends deliciously with oranges, apples, dried fruits like raisins and prunes, potatoes, greens, onions, hard-cooked eggs, dill, caraway, rosemary, and parsley. And no other vegetable has the means to contribute such a wonderful color to whatever it's combined with.

INTO THE BASKET

Beet Roots

- Harvest beets before the first killing frost.
- The best quality is obtained when beets are two inches or less in diameter. With many varieties, flavor and texture begin to lessen if the beets are over three inches. Be sure to mark the exact planting date, and note that most beets can be harvested in 60 to 70 days.
- When harvesting, avoid damaging beets by pulling them out by hand, rather than digging with a tool.
- Beets should be smooth and firm when harvested. If beets are older, they may tend to crack and fissure at the top, but harvest them anyway—they're still good to eat.

Beet Leaves

- Harvest greens anytime throughout the season by taking just a few outer leaves from each plant.
- Beet greens are best when they're young and tender, about 6 inches tall.
- Poor-quality beet greens do not necessarily indicate poor-quality beet roots.

Weights and Measures

1 pound
    = 10 2-inch-diameter
      beets
    = 2 cups of ½-inch
      beets
4 2-inch-diameter cooked
beets and ⅓ cup of any
liquid
    = 1 cup puree
4 medium uncooked,
shredded beet leaves
    = 2 ounces or 1 cup
One pound of beets, thinly
    sliced and placed in a
    covered dish, will take
    about 8 minutes to cook
    in a microwave.

INDOOR STORAGE

Short-term Storage

- Beets can be stored in the refrigerator for a few weeks. Twist off the tops and put the beets in plastic bags. Leave the bags open so moisture does not build up inside.
- Beet greens will also keep, wrapped and refrigerated, for about a week.

Long-term Storage

- Don't wash beets before storage. Gently twist off tops, leaving about two inches of stem. If leaves are left on, they will drain moisture from the roots, causing them to shrivel. To prevent beets from drying out, store them in a single layer, stem-side up, in sand, peat moss, or sawdust in an area close to 32°F and 90 to 95 percent humidity. Basements or root cellars are, of course, good choices. Make sure the beets do not touch each other. Beets stored this way will keep for up to five months, depending on the variety.
- To freeze beets, cut, slice, or grate them and store in freezer bags. Thaw before using in recipes that call for fresh beets.
- To freeze beet greens, wash them, dry thoroughly, and trim stems. Stack the leaves, flat, between squares of waxed paper. Seal stacks in plastic bags and freeze. Defrost before using.

CULINARY TECHNIQUES

Tips to Minimize Bleeding

- Gently twist tops off. Don't cut them.
- Wash beets gently so skin doesn't tear and rootlets don't break.
- Add a dash of vinegar to the cooking water.
- When adding beets to recipes, bake instead of boiling them.

Peeling Tips

- Beet skins come off easiest when they are still hot. As soon as you can handle them, plunge into cold water. Skins should slip right off.
- When pureeing beets, don't bother peeling, just scrub the skins with a brush. The peels will dissolve when pureed, and you'll be adding fiber to your diet.

■■■ OK, NEXT YEAR ■■■

- Want a beet that won't bleed? Grow Burpee's Golden Beet.
- Long-storage beets include Lutz Greenleaf (also called Long Season and Winter Keeper), Perfect Detroit, Always Tender, and Detroit Dark Red.
- Fast-maturing varieties include Earlisweet, Extra Early, Ruby Queen, Early Wonder, Warnor, Flat Egyptian, Little Egypt, First Crop, and Early Red Ball.
- If you're looking for an extra-sweet beet, try Sweetheart, Mono King, Red Ace, or Big Red.
- Beets famous for their vitamin-rich greens include Beets for Greens, Green Top Bunching, Tendersweet, Cut and Come Again, Early Wonder, German Lutz, and Lutz Green Leaf.
- Nonfibrous white varieties include Snowhite, Klein Wanzelbei's, Burpee White, and Albino White.
- Monogerm is a variety that needs no thinning—one beet grows from each seed.
- Grow carrot-shaped beets for easy slicing. Varieties include Cylindrica, Formanova, and Crapaudine.
- Baby beets are best for canning. Try Baby Canning, Baby Beet, Badger Baby, or Best of All.

tip

Beet Puree

Beet puree can be frozen for up to 2 months. Simply cook whole beets until tender, puree until smooth in a food processor or blender, and store tightly covered in freezer containers or ice cube trays. Thaw before using.

Add basil, dill, rosemary, or chives to beet puree, heat through, and serve with roast chicken or pork.

Try beet puree or grated beets in dessert recipes calling for pureed or grated carrots or zucchini.

Crimson Cocktail

2 servings

1 cup apple juice
1 cinnamon stick
1 slice (¼ inch thick) ginger root
1 whole clove
2 cups chilled beet juice (the liquid left over when beets are
      cooked)

In a small saucepan, combine apple juice, cinnamon stick, ginger, and clove. Bring to a boil. Reduce heat to low and simmer for 10 minutes. Remove from heat, let cool, and then chill thoroughly.

Remove cinnamon stick, ginger, and clove. Combine apple juice and beet juice and stir to blend thoroughly.

tip

Red Beet Eggs

Great for picnics and barbecues.

To a large glass jar, add peeled hard-cooked eggs, sliced raw onions, and a couple of whole cloves. Fill the jar with half vinegar and half beet juice (the liquid left over when beets are cooked). Cover the jar and refrigerate. They'll keep for 3 months.

Ruby Beet Dip

makes about 1 cup

Great for stuffing celery.

½ cup low-fat cottage cheese
½ cup plain yogurt
¼ cup beet puree (page 15)
2 teaspoons lemon juice
1 clove garlic, minced
1 tablespoon minced fresh parsley
1 tablespoon minced fresh chives
⅛ teaspoon crumbled dried savory
½ teaspoon caraway seeds (optional)

Whip cottage cheese until smooth in a blender or food processor. Add remaining ingredients and blend thoroughly.

Beets with Mustard Sauce

4 servings

1½ tablespoons butter
1½ tablespoons whole wheat flour
½ cup chicken stock
½ cup milk
1 tablespoon Dijon mustard
2 teaspoons minced fresh chives
⅛ teaspoon dried tarragon
6 medium-size cooked beets, sliced

In a small saucepan, melt butter over medium-low heat. Stir in flour and cook, stirring constantly, for 1 or 2 minutes. Remove pan from heat. Whisk in stock and milk gradually. Return pan to low heat and cook, whisking constantly, until mixture thickens and comes to a boil. Simmer for 1 minute. Remove from heat. Blend in mustard, chives, and tarragon. Arrange beets on a heated platter and serve warm accompanied by the mustard sauce.

Variation: Mound beets in center of round platter. Surround with other cooked vegetables such as parsnips, carrots, potatoes, leeks, turnips, or whatever you have on hand. Alternate colors for an attractive display.

No-Fat Soups

Beet puree will thicken soup without the addition of butter or flour. Use about ⅓ cup of beet puree for 2 cups of soup, stirred in and simmered for at least 10 minutes. This is a particularly nice idea for chilled summer soups, such as gazpacho, or for cabbage soup, thick tomato-based soups, or vegetable cream soups.

Beet, Orange, and Watercress Salad

4 servings

2 cups julienned beets
2 tablespoons olive oil
1 tablespoon tarragon wine or white wine vinegar
1 bunch watercress, stems removed
½ cup thinly sliced red onions
1 large orange, separated into sections, then broken into pieces

Place beets in a small bowl. Whisk together oil and vinegar in a separate bowl. Toss 2 tablespoons of dressing with beets. Let stand at room temperature for 1 hour.

Wash and dry watercress. Place on a flat serving dish. Arrange onion slices and orange slices around edge of plate over watercress. Pour remaining dressing over watercress mixture.

Immediately before serving, place beets in center of watercress.

tip

Stuffed Beets

Bake beets in a pan with ½ inch of water at 400°F for 1 hour. Peel them, then hollow them out with a melon baller. (Use the hollowed-out parts to toss into vegetable soups or to make beet puree.) Stuff with egg salad, tuna salad, bean salad, or marinated minced vegetables. Use larger stuffed beets as appetizers and smaller ones to garnish platters.

Apricot-Glazed Beets

4 servings

2 tablespoons butter
1 teaspoon lemon juice
¼ cup maple syrup
¼ cup apricot juice*
⅛ teaspoon freshly grated nutmeg
⅛ teaspoon grated ginger root (optional)
12 to 16 baby beets, ½ to 1 inch in diameter, cooked

In a medium-size saucepan, combine butter, lemon juice, maple syrup, apricot juice, nutmeg, and ginger. Bring to a boil over medium heat. Reduce heat to low and simmer for 4 to 8 minutes. Add beets and gently toss to coat. Heat through for 1 minute.

*To make your own apricot juice: Combine ¼ cup dried apricots and 1 cup water in a small saucepan. Bring to a boil. Reduce heat, cover, and simmer over very low heat for about 40 minutes, or until apricots are soft. Remove apricots (these can be diced and sprinkled over beets).

Beet Pasta

makes about 1 pound, or enough for 4 people

1 cup whole wheat flour
1 cup (or slightly more) unbleached white flour
2 eggs
¼ cup beet puree (page 15)
1 teaspoon olive oil
3 to 6 tablespoons beet juice (the liquid left over when beets are
    cooked) or water

In a large bowl, combine whole wheat flour and white flour. Make a well in the center and break eggs into the well. With a fork, beat eggs lightly. Stir in puree and oil. With a circular motion, begin to draw flour from the sides. Add a tablespoon of beet juice and continue mixing. Add enough beet juice to moisten all the flour. When dough becomes too stiff to mix with a fork, use your hands. Pat into a ball. Clean and slightly flour the work surface. Knead dough for 5 to 8 minutes, or until no longer sticky. Dough should be

Freezer Beets

Frozen raw or cooked beets will retain their intense color and pungent flavor for up to 3 months. Raw beets will also keep their crisp texture. Here are some ways to use them:

- Sauté raw beets alone or combine with other vegetables. For example, julienne beets and carrots.
- Slice beets into finger-size sticks before freezing. Thaw and serve with dips.
- Use as garnish for soups or salads.
- Simmer cooked beets with sliced apples until they are soft and mixture has thickened. Season with nutmeg or mace and serve as an accompaniment to meats.

smooth and elastic. Sprinkle with a little more flour, if necessary. Let dough rest for 20 minutes, covered, then divide into 4 parts.

With a pasta machine or by hand, roll out one-quarter of the dough at a time, to desired thinness. If you're using a pasta machine, stop at the third from thinnest setting. When all the dough has been rolled, cut into desired width by machine or with a sharp knife.

Cook pasta in a large kettle of boiling water, to which a bit of oil has been added, until al dente, about 3 or 4 minutes. Drain, toss with accompaniments or sauce, and serve.

When serving pasta, try tossing with:

- olive oil, minced garlic, freshly grated Parmesan cheese, freshly ground black pepper, and fresh, uncooked baby peas
- shredded beet leaves, parsley, and grated mozzarella cheese
- sliced sautéed mushrooms, chopped fresh parsley, chopped walnuts, and a bit of walnut oil
- olive oil, chopped fresh tomatoes, minced garlic, and minced fresh basil

To store pasta:

- Dry pasta until stiff. Store in an airtight container. Cooking time will be 7 or 8 minutes.
- Freeze pasta in a plastic bag. To cook, drop frozen pasta right into boiling water. Cooking time will be 5 or 6 minutes.

Pasta Primavera

4 servings

When brought to room temperature or chilled, this makes a terrific pasta salad.

3 tablespoons olive oil
3 cloves garlic, finely minced
½ small dried hot red pepper, broken in half
1 tablespoon minced fresh parsley
½ teaspoon dried oregano
⅓ cup lightly steamed julienned carrots
⅓ cup lightly steamed small new peas
2 cups julienned beets
¼ cup grated Parmesan cheese
1 pound linguine, cooked

In a small saucepan, heat oil over low heat. Add garlic and pepper and cook until garlic is golden, 1 or 2 minutes. Stir in parsley and oregano. Remove from heat and allow to cool a few minutes.

In a warm serving bowl, combine carrots, peas, beets, cheese, and hot linguine. Pour sauce over and toss to combine. Serve immediately.

Ideas for Beet Salads

Raw beets are irresistible both in flavor and in texture. Julienne them, slice them into coins, grate them, or shave them into curls with a vegetable peeler. Then use as garnishes or toss into salads. For instance, you can combine:

- diced beets, diced tart apples, green grapes, celery, and chives
- beets with shredded spinach, mushrooms, and a dash of grated lime peel
- minced beets, tiny pasta, and rosemary as a stuffing for tomatoes or artichokes
- beets with carrots, ground cumin, fresh parsley, and lemon juice
- beets and caraway with cooked onions, leeks, and rice
- shredded raw beets with diagonally cut asparagus, watercress, and fresh tarragon
- shredded beet leaves with other salad greens

Stuffed Beet Leaves

6 servings

30 beet leaves, washed thoroughly
 1 tablespoon olive oil
¼ cup minced shallots
 1 clove garlic, minced
 3 tablespoons chopped pine nuts
 1 pound lean ground pork (beef, lamb, or veal may be
        substituted)
¾ cup cooked brown rice
 1 egg, beaten
 2 tablespoons grated Parmesan cheese
 2 tablespoons minced fresh parsley
 2 teaspoons minced fresh rosemary or ½ teaspoon crumbled
        dried rosemary
 1 to 1½ cups chicken stock
 1 small onion, chopped
 1 small carrot, chopped
½ stalk celery, chopped
⅓ cup chopped canned tomatoes
½ bay leaf
1½ teaspoons minced fresh thyme or ½ teaspoon dried thyme

Blanch beet leaves for 5 seconds in boiling water (using a triple-mesh strainer makes it easier). Immediately place under cold running water. Drain and then place on paper towels to dry thoroughly.

Heat oil in a deep skillet. Add shallots and garlic and sauté until soft, 3 or 4 minutes. Add pine nuts and sauté for 1 minute. Add pork and cook until no longer pink, stirring frequently and breaking up large pieces. Remove from heat. Stir in rice, egg, cheese, parsley, and rosemary.

In a casserole, heat 1 cup of the stock. Add onions, carrots, and celery. Cook, stirring frequently, until vegetables are tender, about 10 minutes. Stir in tomatoes, bay leaf, and thyme.

Place a beet leaf on a flat surface. Place 1 teaspoonful of pork mixture in center. Fold up bottom, then sides, then top of leaf to enclose filling. Place on top of vegetables in casserole. Repeat with remaining leaves. Cover dish tightly with aluminum foil. Bake in a preheated 350°F oven for 30 to 35 minutes, or until leaves are tender. Add more stock if it seems to be drying up.

CHAPTER 3

CABBAGE

Cabbage is not just another pretty face in the garden. It is especially outstanding as a source of vitamin C and is rich in dietary fiber, too.

You can help retain these nutrients in head-type cabbage by steaming, rather than boiling. Steaming also preserves more of cabbage's texture than boiling does. Most head types can be quartered and steamed for about 10 minutes, although winter and red varieties may take a bit more time.

Choy-type cabbages are like two vegetables in one, each requiring different cooking techniques. The stalks, for instance, are used like celery and are sliced and stir-fried or chopped raw and tossed into salads. The leaves are treated like spinach or chard and can even be stuffed with rice and vegetables, rolled into tiny cigars, and steamed.

INTO THE BASKET

- Cabbage can be harvested any time after the heads have formed and they are firm to the touch (like a softball). Be sure to harvest before a hard frost. With a sharp knife, cut the heads off of the root system. Cutting high on the stem encourages a second growth in some varieties.
- Early varieties will yield a second harvest if stalks and roots are left undisturbed. When little buds have resprouted along the stalks, remove all but one or two, and they will develop into small, delicious heads by winter.
- If you want to hold cabbage instead of harvesting immediately, twist the head to break some—but not all—of the roots. Cutting close to the plant with a spade or shovel works, too.

INDOOR STORAGE

Short-term Storage

Store whole heads in a moist plastic bag in the refrigerator. They'll last for up to two weeks.

23

tip

Freezer Heads

Cut cabbages into 2-inch chunks and blanch in boiling water for 3 minutes. Quickly plunge into ice water, pat dry, and pack in airtight freezer bags.

To use, take chunks directly from the freezer and simmer in stock or tomato sauce until defrosted and heated through.

▰▰▰ OK, NEXT YEAR ▰▰▰

- Avoid cracked heads by watering regularly. (Cabbage needs about one inch of water per week, except when growing in heavy, water-retentive soils.)
- Late varieties store better than early types and tend to taste sweeter because they mature in cooler fall temperatures.
- Prevent disease and overwintering pests by rotating crops from year to year. Cabbage may be planted in soil previously planted to beans, lettuce, onions, corn, or peas.
- Early-maturing varieties include Golden Acre, Salarite, and Early Jersey Wakefield, which has a conical head.
- For smaller plots, choose miniature, dwarf, or compact head varieties like Morden Dwarf, Jersey Wakefield, and Emerald Cross.
- Late varieties tend to crack less and are good winter keepers. Try Danish Ballhead, Late Flat Dutch, Penn State Ballhead, Wisconsin All Seasons, Wisconsin Hollander, Chieftain Savoy, and Hybrid Savoy King.
- Disease-resistant varieties include Sanibel, Market Prize, Market Topper, Golden Acre, Early Jersey Wakefield (conical head), Gourmet, and Prime Pac.
- Grow giant cabbages by planting Heavy Weighter or Jumbo. The more room you give cabbage, the larger it will grow.

Long-term Storage

- Discard the inferior outer leaves of cabbages and check for insects. Take care not to bruise the heads or rotting could occur.
- Firm heads will keep for up to six months at 32° to 40°F and a moist 90 percent humidity. Be sure to lay them out so they're not touching.
- Late white and red varieties will last for several months when hung upside down in a shed or garage. Trim off the floppy outer leaves, but keep the inner leaves and roots intact for hanging.
- If you have a cool but dry storage area, wrap heads loosely in plastic wrap to retain moisture.

CULINARY TECHNIQUES

- If you cut into a head and find a yellow ring above the core, that part is going to taste hot and bitter. Avoid those flavors by eating only the outside of the head.

- If you find the cooking odor of cabbage to be too strong, toss an English walnut or a stalk of celery into the pot. Long cooking also encourages strong cabbage odors, so choose a quick and healthful cooking method, like steaming.

Tiny Cabbage Rolls

makes about 80 rolls

1 medium-size head savoy cabbage
1 large onion, chopped
2 tablespoons corn oil
1 tablespoon whole wheat flour
1 cup water or chicken stock
1½ pounds mixed ground beef, pork, and veal
3 eggs
½ teaspoon dry mustard
½ cup cooked brown rice
  freshly ground black pepper to taste
2 cups tomato sauce
2 cups canned whole tomatoes, pureed in a blender
1½ teaspoons Dijon mustard
¼ cup molasses

Remove core from cabbage. Steam cabbage until leaves can be removed, about 15 minutes (do not overcook). Drain cabbage leaves on paper towels.

In a small nonstick skillet, cook onions in hot oil until tender, about 5 minutes. Remove with a slotted spoon. Add flour to skillet and cook, stirring constantly, for 1 or 2 minutes, or until browned. Add water or stock and cook until thickened (makes a brown roux).

In a large bowl, combine ground meat, eggs, dry mustard, rice, pepper, onions, and half of the roux. Mix thoroughly.

Cut large cabbage leaves into 4 pieces and smaller leaves into 2 pieces. Place a small portion of meat mixture at base of each leaf and roll, tucking in the ends. Set rolls aside while you prepare sauce.

In a small saucepan, combine tomato sauce, pureed tomatoes, Dijon mustard, molasses, and remaining roux. Simmer until warmed. Pour into a large casserole and place cabbage rolls in sauce. Cover dish with aluminum foil and bake in a preheated 350°F oven for 1 to 1¼ hours. Serve warm or cold.

Variation: Omit ground meat. Use about 3½ cups cooked rice.

tip

Don't discard those vitamin C-packed cabbage cores. Instead, grate or shred them and toss with minced scallions, capers, and a dressing of 1 part plain yogurt to 1 part mayonnaise.

Chinese Hot and Sour Soup

4 servings

  4 cups chicken stock
2½ cups finely shredded cabbage
  ¼ cup finely shredded bamboo shoots
  1 tablespoon soy sauce
  ¼ pound lean boneless pork, finely shredded (about ½ cup)
  1 teaspoon finely minced ginger root
  3 cloves garlic, minced
  ¼ teaspoon white pepper
  2 tablespoons rice or cider vinegar
  2 tablespoons cornstarch, mixed with ¼ cup cold water
  1 egg, slightly beaten
  1 teaspoon sesame oil
  ¼ to ½ teaspoon chili oil
  1 scallion (including greens), minced

In a 3-quart saucepan, combine stock, cabbage, bamboo shoots, and soy sauce. Bring to a boil over moderate heat. Add pork, ginger, and garlic, stirring to separate pork. Reduce heat to low, cover, and simmer for 4 minutes. Add pepper and vinegar. Slowly bring to a boil. Stir cornstarch mixture to recombine and pour into soup. Stir a few seconds until soup thickens. Slowly pour in beaten egg, stirring gently. Remove from heat. Ladle into a serving bowl. Stir in sesame and chili oils and sprinkle with scallions.

Variation: Use half shredded cooked chicken and half pork, or use all chicken.

Crisp and Creamy Cabbage

4 servings

1½ to 2 cups chicken stock
  1 medium-size head cabbage, cut into 8 wedges
  ½ cup half-and-half
  1 tablespoon butter
  ½ teaspoon freshly grated nutmeg, or to taste
  ⅛ teaspoon freshly ground white pepper, or to taste

Pour enough stock into a medium-size skillet to measure ½ inch. Bring to a boil. Add cabbage wedges. Reduce heat and cook, covered, until cabbage is crisp-tender, about 5 minutes. Remove cabbage with a slotted spoon to a warm serving dish. Pour off all but 2 tablespoons of the stock from skillet. Add half-and-half and butter. Heat gently (do not boil) until thoroughly warm. Stir in nutmeg and pepper. Pour over cabbage wedges.

Note: For a reduced calorie version, substitute milk for the half-and-half.

tip

Use raw cabbage leaves to scoop up tiny appetizer meatballs, kabobs, sandwich fillings, chunks of cheese and mustard, marinated vegetables, and pasta salad.

Old-Fashioned Cabbage Soup

makes about 2 quarts

1 large onion, thinly sliced
2 medium-size carrots, diced
1 stalk celery, diced
1 parsnip, diced
1 medium-size turnip, peeled and diced
1 small head cabbage, coarsely shredded
8 to 10 cups beef stock
    bouquet garni—6 sprigs parsley, 2 unpeeled cloves garlic, 1 bay
        leaf, 4 black peppercorns, and 3 sprigs thyme (or ½
        teaspoon dried thyme), gathered together in a piece of
        cheesecloth and tied with string
1 large potato, peeled and diced
1 medium-size tomato, peeled, seeded, and diced

Combine onions, carrots, celery, parsnips, turnips, cabbage, and 8 cups of the stock in an 8-quart pot. Add bouquet garni. Bring to a boil. Reduce heat and simmer, partially covered, for 45 minutes. Add potatoes and tomatoes and cook for 20 to 30 minutes, or until all vegetables are tender (add more stock if necessary to keep vegetables covered). Discard bouquet garni. Serve immediately.

Variations:

Cut ½ pound turkey sausage into 1-inch rounds. Brown in a skillet. Add to soup during last 10 minutes of cooking time.

Add 1 cup cooked or canned white beans (Great Northern, marrow, or navy) during last 5 minutes of cooking time.

Chinese Cabbage

This hardy, cool-weather crop comes in both heading and nonheading varieties. Heading varieties include Michihli, Chihfu, and Wong Bok, and nonheading favorites are Pak Choi and Taisai.

To harvest and store, pull up the entire plant, roots and all. Wrap the plants in several thicknesses of brown paper or newspaper, and store upright in a wastebasket or cardboard box. If you place in a cool cellar or garage, Chinese cabbage will last about a month.

Use Chinese cabbage ribs and leaves in stir fries, omelets, or sautéed with tomatoes, garlic, and scallions. Use the ribs in soups, stews, and casseroles; the leaves can be stuffed like other cabbages.

Caraway Coleslaw

makes about 6 cups

Coleslaw:
6 cups shredded cabbage
1 carrot, shredded
2 scallions, minced
⅓ cup diced celery
⅓ cup slivered green or red peppers

Dressing:
½ cup buttermilk
3 tablespoons mayonnaise
1 tablespoon white wine vinegar
1 teaspoon honey
   pinch of paprika
½ teaspoon caraway seeds, lightly crushed in a mortar
        or spice grinder

To prepare the coleslaw: In a large bowl, combine cabbage, carrot, scallions, celery, and peppers. Mix well.

To prepare the dressing: In a small bowl, whisk together buttermilk, mayonnaise, vinegar, honey, paprika, and caraway seeds.

Pour dressing over cabbage mixture and toss well. Chill thoroughly for at least 1 hour.

Variation: To make celery coleslaw, substitute celery seeds for the caraway seeds and add a dash of dry mustard.

tip

For a delicious instant salad, pack a wedge of fresh cabbage with your lunch. No utensils needed!

Curried Cabbage, Lemon, and Rice Salad

4 to 6 servings

Salad:
3 cups finely shredded cabbage
1½ cups cooked, cooled brown rice
2 scallions, thinly sliced
⅓ cup minced sweet red peppers
¼ cup cooked fresh or thawed frozen peas
2 tablespoons minced fresh parsley

Dressing:
2 tablespoons lemon juice
½ teaspoon curry powder
⅛ teaspoon ground ginger
⅛ teaspoon ground cinnamon
pinch of cayenne pepper
¼ cup corn oil

To prepare the salad: In a large bowl, combine cabbage, rice, scallions, peppers, peas, and parsley. Mix well.

To prepare the dressing: In a small bowl, whisk together lemon juice, curry powder, ginger, cinnamon, and cayenne. Slowly whisk in oil.

Pour dressing over cabbage mixture and toss well. Chill thoroughly.

tip

Cabbage as Stuffing

Shred cabbage, then mix with an egg and enough milk or stock to moisten the mixture. Then add:

- corn-bread crumbs, chopped pecans, minced onions, and ground nutmeg
- cracker crumbs, minced garlic, fennel, and grated parsnip
- rice, wild or tame mushrooms, and tarragon

Use to stuff fish, meatloaf, poultry, game, or vegetables.

Ideas for Cabbage-Roll Stuffings

Blanch cabbage leaves in boiling water until they are flexible but not mushy. Pat dry, then fill them with:

- cooked cracked wheat, sautéed leeks, Swiss cheese, and caraway
- tomatoes, minced onions, minced green peppers, cooked rice, thyme, and oregano
- shredded spinach, crumbled feta cheese, bread crumbs, and minced fresh mint
- cooked ground chicken, toasted pine nuts, crushed or minced garlic, and rosemary
- corn kernels (uncooked), grated carrots, mashed potatoes, fresh chives, and fresh dill
- cooked barley, sautéed chopped mushrooms, sautéed chopped onions, and minced dried currants
- cooked elbow macaroni, grated cheddar cheese, chopped apples, and ground mace

Simmer the stuffed rolls in stock in a skillet until heated through. Serve warm or cold.

Whole Stuffed Cabbage

8 servings

1 large head cabbage, preferably savoy
¼ pound spinach
2 tablespoons safflower oil
½ cup minced onions
2 shallots, minced
¼ cup minced carrots
1 cup finely chopped cooked chicken
1 cup fresh whole grain bread crumbs
2 tablespoons minced fresh parsley
½ teaspoon soy sauce
2 eggs, beaten
¼ teaspoon freshly grated nutmeg
6 cups chicken stock
1 clove unpeeled garlic
½ stalk celery
1 small onion
    bouquet garni—4 sprigs parsley, 1 bay leaf, and 3 sprigs thyme (or ½ teaspoon dried thyme), gathered together in a piece of cheesecloth and tied with string

Trim stem end of cabbage and remove any damaged leaves. Steam for 10 minutes or until outer leaves can be pulled back. Place cabbage on a piece of cheesecloth. Gently pull back leaves to expose heart. Carefully cut heart out and reserve, leaving outer leaves attached. Place cheesecloth with cabbage into a bowl.

Blanch and finely chop spinach (will yield about 1/4 cup). Set aside.

In a small skillet, heat oil. Add onions, shallots, and carrots, and sauté until soft, about 5 minutes. Turn into a medium-size bowl. Add chicken, spinach, bread crumbs, parsley, soy sauce, eggs, and nutmeg, and mix well. Finely chop cabbage heart and add to chicken mixture.

Pack stuffing into cabbage center, shaping mixture like cabbage heart. Detach 2 leaves (or use any that fell off during steaming), and press over stuffing. Fold all remaining leaves back into place and overlap them to completely enclose stuffing. Pull up edges of cheesecloth and tie at top.

In a large pot, bring 4 cups of the stock, garlic, celery, onion, and bouquet garni to a boil. Lower cabbage into stock. Reduce heat and simmer, partially covered, for 1½ to 2 hours, or until cabbage is tender. Remove cabbage by inserting prongs of a fork through top of bag and lifting cabbage and cheesecloth out. Drain in a colander for 10 minutes. Remove to a bowl and cut open cheesecloth. Lay a plate on top of cabbage and turn over. Lift off bowl and remove cheesecloth. Place bowl over cabbage again and invert plate and bowl. Serve in bowl. Cut into wedges and spoon some cooking liquid over each serving.

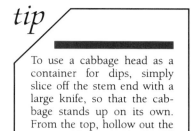

tip

To use a cabbage head as a container for dips, simply slice off the stem end with a large knife, so that the cabbage stands up on its own. From the top, hollow out the center with a paring knife and melon baller. Fill with dip and serve with raw vegetables. Save the scooped-out portion and use in slaws, soups, or stuffings.

Dutch Spiced Red Cabbage

makes about 7 pints

  3 quarts red wine vinegar
  1 large onion, thinly sliced and separated
½ cup apple juice
  1 teaspoon celery seeds
  1 teaspoon freshly ground black pepper
  1 teaspoon freshly grated nutmeg
  1 teaspoon freshly ground allspice
  1 teaspoon ground cinnamon
  5 bay leaves
½ cup honey
12 cups red cabbage, shredded

In an 8-quart pot, boil vinegar for 8 minutes with onions, apple juice, celery seeds, pepper, nutmeg, allspice, cinnamon, and bay leaves. Add honey. Add cabbage to pot and simmer for 15 minutes.

Drain cabbage and save liquid.

To can: Pack cabbage in sterilized pint jars. Pour hot liquid over cabbage, allowing ¼-inch headspace. Adjust lids and process in a boiling-water bath for 15 minutes.

Variation: To make this recipe without using your stove (sun cabbage), place shredded red cabbage into a large glass bowl and place in the direct sun for 3 hours. Stir through occasionally. At the end of 3 hours, pour off any liquid that may have accumulated.

Combine vinegar with apple juice and spices. Simmer for 8 to 10 minutes, then add honey. Drain cabbage and save liquid. Follow canning directions above.

Oven-Crisped Spring Rolls

makes 12 rolls

    1 medium-size head cabbage, shredded
    8 scallions, minced
    4 shiitake mushrooms, soaked for 20 minutes and minced
    2 tablespoons sesame seeds
    2 teaspoons soy sauce
    1 teaspoon honey
    1 teaspoon sesame oil
    2 teaspoons cornstarch
    1 tablespoon peanut butter
   ⅛ teaspoon ground ginger
  12 spring rolls or egg-roll skins
    1 teaspoon cornstarch, mixed with 1 tablespoon cold water
    1 tablespoon safflower oil

Preheat oven to 475°F.

To prepare the filling: In a large bowl, combine cabbage, scallions, mushrooms, sesame seeds, soy sauce, honey, sesame oil, 2 teaspoons cornstarch, peanut butter, and ginger.

Place a spring roll or egg-roll skin on the counter with a corner facing you. About 2 inches from the corner, shape ¼ cup of filling into a horizontal log. Begin to roll by pulling the corner facing you over the log and folding in the sides as you go. When the filling is covered, wet remaining edges with cornstarch mixture and continue rolling and folding sides in. Place on an oiled cookie sheet and continue with remaining skins and filling.

Brush spring rolls with oil (you may not need full tablespoon) and bake for 8 minutes. Flip spring rolls over and bake for 5 minutes more, or until slightly puffed and dotted with golden brown.

Variations:

Substitute 4 large button mushrooms for the shiitake mushrooms, if you prefer.

Substitute ½ cup of finely minced cooked meat, chicken, fish, or shrimp for half of the cabbage.

Sauté of Cabbage and Apples

4 servings

2 teaspoons olive oil
2 teaspoons butter
1 medium-size leek (white and light green parts only), chopped
6 cups finely sliced cabbage
1 medium unpeeled apple, diced
½ teaspoon crumbled dried savory
    freshly ground black pepper to taste

Heat oil and butter in a large, heavy skillet over medium heat. Add leeks and sauté until soft. Add cabbage and cook, stirring constantly, for 5 or 6 minutes, or until just tender. Add apples, savory, and pepper, and cook until apples are tender, about 2 minutes.

Variation: Spoon into a shallow casserole or gratin dish. Top with ¼ cup moist whole grain bread crumbs or grated sharp cheddar cheese. Bake in a preheated 375°F oven until top is browned.

CHAPTER 4

CARROTS

Carrots appear in abundant variety, but when you come face to face with them in the kitchen, there are really only two types: young and tender, and older and tougher. Chances are, if you grow your own carrots, you'll have plenty of the young and tender ones that can be enjoyed without peeling or cooking. Older carrots should be peeled using a swivel-blade peeler. This kind (as opposed to a stationary-blade peeler) is easier to control and glides freely over uneven surfaces. Additionally, it removes only a thin layer of skin, leaving more vegetable and more nutrients.

INTO THE BASKET

- Carrots are ready to eat when they're two inches or longer. Harvest them when they are the size that you prefer.
- To harvest, grab the greens near the ground and pull. Moist soil will make harvesting easier, but if the soil is heavy, use a trowel to help remove the root.
- Generally, the darker the greens, the bigger the carrot.

INDOOR STORAGE

Short-term Storage

- Seal carrots without their greens in plastic bags and they'll keep, refrigerated, for about a month.
- Carrot greens are edible and will keep for about five days if they are sprayed with water and sealed in a plastic bag.

Long-term Storage

- Cut stems to about an inch and let unwashed carrots cure in full sun for about two hours.
- Fill a plastic trash can (or strong cardboard box) with alternate layers of unbruised carrots and sand, sawdust, or peat.

Make sure the carrots aren't touching each other. Cover the can to keep the carrots from drying out, and store the can in a cool, airy place. The carrots will keep for about six months.
- Don't store carrots with apples. The ethylene that apples give off as they ripen could make the carrots taste bitter.

CULINARY TECHNIQUES

Easy Slices and Julienne Strips

If you've ever tried to slice a carrot lengthwise into slices and instead it rolled off the cutting board, try this. Cut a thin lengthwise slice from the side of the carrot, turn and cut another slice and continue two more times, until the carrot is no longer round, but has four corners. Now you can slice or julienne with impunity.

More Flavor

The Chinese slice their carrots for stir fries and soups on a diagonal, which exposes more surface and therefore gives more flavor.

Weights and Measures

1 pound carrots, shredded
   = 4 cups
1 pound carrots, juiced
   = 1 cup
3 medium-size carrots,
cooked and pureed
   = 1 cup puree
2 medium-size carrots,
shredded
   = 1 cup
2 medium-size carrots, cut
into coins
   = 1 cup

▰▰ OK, NEXT YEAR ▰▰

- Loose, rock-free soil is important for growing good carrots. A fertile, well-drained, sandy loam that's low in nitrogen will give your carrots an easy time.
- Small varieties suited to growing in heavy soils include Oxheart, Kundulas Kinko, and Short 'n Sweet, which are round; Planet and Gold Nugget, which are beet-shaped; and Goldinhart and Little Finger, which are conventionally shaped but small.
- Good keepers include Scarlet Keeper, Nantes Forto, Chantenay, Danvers, and Oxheart.
- Avoid bitter-tasting carrots by giving them an even supply of water and nutrients, particularly potassium.
- Companion planting with rosemary, sage, or coriander may help avoid carrot rust flies. These herbs also make good culinary companions to carrots.
- Planting buckwheat and white mustard in the bed where you will later plant carrots can help ward off wireworm. Turn under the buckwheat or mustard two weeks before planting carrots.
- Carrots good for canning, freezing, and juicing include Touchon, Redheart, Park's Munchy Hybrid, Nantes Coreless, Tendersweet, Scarlet Coreless (Early Coreless), Burpee's Gold Pak, and Nantes Half Long. Note that these coreless varieties do not store well.

Carrot Coins
with Chicken and Feta

8 servings

 3 large, thick carrots
½ cup ground cooked chicken
½ cup grated Swiss cheese
¼ cup crumbled feta cheese
 1 clove garlic, minced
 1 tablespoon minced fresh dill
 2 tablespoons dry, whole grain bread crumbs
   dill or parsley sprigs for garnish

Cut off thickest part of each carrot (reserve rest for another use). Steam carrot pieces for 5 minutes or until crisp-tender. Drain and cool. Slice carrot pieces into ¼-inch rounds, or slice diagonally into thin pieces (if you have flower cookie cutters, use these to make decorative shapes).

In a small bowl, mix together chicken, cheeses, garlic, and dill. Top each carrot slice with a teaspoon of chicken mixture. Sprinkle with bread crumbs. Place on a cookie sheet.

Broil until topping is very hot and cheese has melted. Serve immediately, garnished with dill or parsley.

Carrots with Citrus and Jalapeño

4 servings

 1 pound carrots, cut into julienne strips
 1 jalapeño pepper, seeded and minced
   juice of 1 lemon
   juice of 1 lime
¼ teaspoon honey
½ teaspoon coriander seeds, crushed

Set carrots in a strainer and pour boiling water over them for about 5 seconds.

In a medium-size bowl, toss carrots with jalapeño. In a small bowl, combine the 2 juices, honey, and coriander. Pour over carrots and toss 30 times. Serve at room temperature or chilled.

Carrot Turbans Stuffed with Shrimp

8 to 10 servings

 3 large, thick carrots
½ pound medium-size shrimp
 1 tablespoon milk
    dash of cayenne pepper
 3 ounces cream cheese, softened
¼ teaspoon Dijon mustard
¼ teaspoon tomato paste
    lemon juice to taste
    dill or parsley sprigs for garnish

Using a vegetable peeler, cut wide strips lengthwise from each carrot. Blanch for 30 seconds in boiling water. Drain, then plunge carrot strips into ice water. Dry on paper towels.

In a saucepan of boiling water, boil shrimp, covered, over high heat for 3 minutes. Drain. Shell and devein. Chop.

In a food processor or blender, puree ¼ cup of the shrimp with milk and cayenne. Spoon into a bowl. Add cream cheese, mustard, tomato paste, and lemon juice, and mix well. Stir in remaining shrimp.

Place 1 teaspoon of the filling on one end of a carrot strip. Roll up and fasten with toothpicks, if necessary. Repeat with remaining carrot strips. Chill well and remove toothpicks before serving. Garnish with dill or parsley.

tip

Two Easy Carrot Garnishes

Carrot Flowers. Before slicing a carrot into coins, make 3 to 5 small V-shaped cuts down the length of the carrot. Remove the strips that you've made from cutting, and what's left will form the petals. Slice and use as you would carrot coins.

Tiny Carrot Cups. Peel a fat carrot and slice off the top so it's flat. Holding the carrot in one hand with the flat end down, make a diagonal cut starting about 1 inch above the flat end aiming toward the center, stopping when you get there. Make 2 more identical cuts around the circumference of the carrot. When you reach the center on the last cut, a little cup will fall into your hand. Flatten the end and start another cup. Fill the cups with individual servings of sauce, mustard for a cheese tray, herb butter, or cheese spread.

Carrots and Broccoli
with Vinaigrette

4 servings

   1 pound carrots, cut into 2-inch julienne strips
1½ cups broccoli florets
   3 tablespoons wine vinegar
  ½ teaspoon Dijon mustard
   3 tablespoons olive oil
1½ teaspoons minced fresh parsley
1½ teaspoons minced fresh chives
1½ teaspoons minced fresh tarragon or ½ teaspoon dried tarragon
1½ teaspoons minced fresh chervil or ½ teaspoon dried chervil

    Steam carrots and broccoli until tender. Drain and cool. In a small bowl, combine vinegar and mustard. Whisk in oil slowly until emulsified. Stir in herbs.

    Transfer carrots and broccoli to a shallow dish. Pour dressing over vegetables. Serve immediately or let marinate, covered, in refrigerator for 1 or 2 hours.

Creamy Carrot Soup

4 servings

    2 tablespoons butter
    1 pound carrots, cut into ¼-inch coins
    2 cups chicken stock or water, divided
    2 tablespoons brown rice
    2 sprigs thyme or ¼ teaspoon dried thyme
    1 bay leaf
      freshly ground white pepper to taste
1¼ to 1¾ cups milk, or more
  ⅛ teaspoon freshly grated nutmeg
      minced fresh chives for garnish

In a medium-size saucepan, melt butter over low heat. Add carrots and sauté for 10 minutes. Stir in 1 cup of stock or water. Bring to a boil. Reduce heat and simmer until carrots are almost tender, about 5 minutes. With a slotted spoon, remove ¼ cup of carrot slices. Stir remaining stock or water, rice, thyme, bay leaf, and pepper into pan. Bring to a boil. Reduce heat, cover, and simmer until rice is tender, about 30 minutes, stirring occasionally. Remove and discard bay leaf and thyme sprigs.

Drain off liquid and reserve. Transfer rice and carrots to a blender and puree until smooth. With the motor running, gradually add cooking liquid and blend until smooth. Return to saucepan. Simmer for 5 minutes. Gradually stir in enough milk to reach desired consistency. Bring almost to a boil, stirring constantly. Stir in reserved carrots and nutmeg. Ladle into bowls and top each serving with minced chives.

Carrots with Angel Hair Pasta

4 servings

    1 tablespoon olive oil
    2 tablespoons butter, divided
  ¼ cup minced shallots
    2 cloves garlic, minced
    1 pound carrots, cut into 2 × ¼-inch pieces
  ½ cup water

⅛ teaspoon freshly ground white pepper
1 dried hot red pepper, broken in half
¾ pound angel hair pasta
2 tablespoons minced fresh basil or 2 teaspoons dried basil
2 tablespoons minced fresh mint or 2 teaspoons dried mint
½ cup grated Parmesan cheese

Heat oil and 1 tablespoon of the butter in a medium-size skillet over medium-low heat. Add shallots and garlic and cook until soft, about 4 minutes. Add carrots, water, white pepper, and red pepper, cover, and increase heat to medium-high. Cook, stirring frequently, until carrots are tender, about 4 minutes. Uncover and cook until most of the liquid has evaporated. Remove red pepper.

When carrots are almost done, cook pasta and drain. Toss with remaining butter, basil, mint, cheese, and carrot mixture.

Sauté of Lamb with Carrot Threads and Raisins

4 servings

½ pound lamb from leg, cut into paper-thin slices
        against the grain
1 teaspoon cornstarch
1 tablespoon malt vinegar
½ teaspoon soy sauce
1 tablespoon white grape juice
2 cloves garlic, minced
1 teaspoon peanut oil
2 tablespoons golden raisins
2 tablespoons black raisins
1 cup coarsely grated carrots
⅓ cup julienned scallions

In a small bowl, toss lamb with cornstarch until combined. Stir in vinegar, soy sauce, grape juice, and garlic, and let mixture marinate for 30 minutes.

In a large nonstick skillet, sauté lamb in oil for about 3 minutes. Add raisins and carrots and sauté for about 1 minute more. Remove from heat, toss in scallions, and serve.

Ideas for Carrot Salads

- sliced carrots tossed with cider vinegar, orange juice, and minced ginger
- grated carrots with chopped tart apples, raisins, toasted almonds, shredded coconut, and plain yogurt
- carrot coins with tuna, walnuts, mayonnaise, and tarragon
- steamed sliced carrots, shredded chicken, minced celery, minced onions, a splash of sesame oil, and lime juice
- shredded carrots, Napa cabbage (or other Chinese cabbage), minced scallions, and shredded daikon radishes with peanut oil and rice vinegar
- grated carrots, turnips, and red cabbage with lemon juice and olive oil
- carrot batons, sliced avocados, and sliced cucumbers with lime juice and olive oil
- chopped steamed carrots, cubed steamed potatoes, chopped artichoke bottoms, and fresh chervil with lemon juice and walnut oil
- grated carrots, grated celeriac (celery root), minced fresh parsley, and mayonnaise

Chunky Carrots
with Parsnips and Scallions

4 servings

  1 pound carrots, cut into 1-inch chunks
½ pound parsnips, cut into 1-inch chunks
  2 tablespoons olive oil
  1 tablespoon minced scallions
  1 clove garlic, minced
  1 tablespoon chopped fresh parsley
  1 tablespoon chopped fresh basil or 1 teaspoon dried basil
      dash of freshly ground black pepper
      pinch of freshly grated nutmeg
  1 teaspoon lemon juice

Steam or parboil carrots and parsnips until just tender. Drain well.

In a medium-size skillet, heat oil over low heat. Add scallions and garlic and cook for 1 minute. Add parsley, basil, pepper, and nutmeg. Add carrots and parsnips and heat through for 1 or 2 minutes, or until coated with oil. Sprinkle with lemon juice.

tip

Carrot Greens

Snip and toss carrot greens into salads, stir fries, or sautés. They add fresh flavor plus valuable nutrients.

Bay Scallops with Carrot Ribbons and Ginger Cream

4 servings

12 small carrots (about 1 pound)
 1 cup half-and-half
 1 cup chicken or fish stock
 3 small slices ginger root
 1 bay leaf
 2 cloves garlic
½ teaspoon Dijon mustard
    pinch of ground ginger
 1 egg yolk
½ teaspoon honey
    freshly ground black pepper
½ pound bay scallops
 1 teaspoon butter

With a swivel-blade vegetable peeler, slice carrots into ribbons. You should have about 2½ cups. Set ribbons in a strainer, pour boiling water over them for about 3 seconds, and set aside while you prepare ginger cream.

In a medium-size saucepan, combine half-and-half, stock, ginger root, bay leaf, and garlic, and bring to a boil. Continue to boil, whisking regularly, until mixture has been reduced by half. This will take about 10 minutes. Remove ginger root, bay leaf, and garlic with a slotted spoon, and add mustard, ground ginger, egg yolk, honey, and pepper. Whisk until combined, continuing to cook sauce until it is thick and creamy. Cover sauce and set aside.

In a medium-size skillet, sauté scallops in butter until opaque, no more than 3 minutes. Add them to sauce and combine well.

Arrange carrot ribbons on a platter or on individual plates and pour scallop mixture on top. Serve immediately.

Variation: Substitute sautéed shrimp for scallops.

tip

Chilling Facts

Although carrots store well in the root cellar, you may find the need to freeze some. Blanch chunks and slices for about 4 minutes and grated carrots for about 2 minutes before packing and freezing.

Carrot and Cheddar Scones

makes about 3 dozen

1 cup whole wheat flour
1 cup unbleached white flour
1 teaspoon baking soda
2 teaspoons cream of tartar
¼ cup butter, softened
1 cup grated cheddar cheese
¼ teaspoon freshly grated nutmeg
1 cup grated carrots
¾ cup buttermilk

Preheat oven to 475°F.

In a large bowl, combine whole wheat flour, white flour, baking soda, cream of tartar, butter, cheese, nutmeg, and carrots. Add buttermilk and knead dough until smooth.

On a floured surface, roll out dough to ¼-inch thickness and cut out 2½-inch rounds. Place them on a lightly oiled baking sheet, dust lightly with flour, and bake for 8 to 10 minutes.

Carrot Macaroons

makes about 3 dozen

1 cup ground almonds
½ teaspoon finely grated orange peel
1 tablespoon flaked coconut
1 egg white, room temperature
2 tablespoons maple syrup, warmed
2 tablespoons honey, warmed
½ teaspoon vanilla extract
¼ teaspoon almond extract
½ cup grated carrots

Combine almonds, orange peel, and coconut in a medium-size bowl.

In a small bowl, beat egg white until soft peaks form. Gradually beat in maple syrup and honey. Fold into almond mixture. Stir in extracts and carrots. Refrigerate dough for 1 hour. Drop by teaspoonfuls onto a baking sheet that has been lined with parchment paper (or line a baking sheet with aluminum foil and spray lightly with vegetable spray).

Bake in a preheated 300°F oven for 15 to 20 minutes, or until golden but not brown. Lift paper or foil off baking sheet and let cookies cool for 5 minutes. Then transfer cookies to a wire rack and let cool completely. Store in a tightly covered container.

Peeling and Nutrition

Peeling removes about 10 percent of a carrot's weight and about 10 percent of its carotene (pro-vitamin A). There's no extra amount of carotene in the skin.

Carrot-Maple Pudding

6 servings

1½ cups milk
⅓ cup maple syrup
½ teaspoon grated orange peel
½ teaspoon ground cinnamon
¼ teaspoon ground ginger
3 eggs, slightly beaten
1 cup pureed cooked carrots

Preheat oven to 325°F.

In a large bowl, combine milk, maple syrup, orange peel, cinnamon, and ginger. Stir thoroughly. Add eggs and carrots. Beat with a spoon until smooth. Pour into a buttered 1- or 1½-quart baking dish. Place dish in a large baking pan and place on center rack of oven. Pour enough very hot water into pan to come halfway up the sides of the dish. Bake for 1 to 1¼ hours, or until a knife inserted near the edge comes out clean. Cool on a rack to room temperature. Serve immediately or cover and chill thoroughly.

Note: Pudding may also be made in 6 4-ounce glass molds and baked for 40 minutes, or until firm.

CHAPTER 5

CORN

Corn, both kernels and meal, was famous in many cuisines long before American colonists discovered it. In Italy, polenta (a sort of corn meal mush) is mixed with cheese and served for breakfast. The Swiss serve their polenta with roast meats, as do Brazilians, who call it *pirao*. Brazilians also add corn kernels to fish soups and shrimp sautés.

Corn breads are found in the ovens of Mexico and Latin America, where they're known as *tortillas*. In India, corn bread is spiced and called *roti*.

West Indians spice their cornmeal, too, and make it into a porridge called *coo-coo*. Creoles create a similar porridge, serve it with chicken livers, and call it *suso*.

INTO THE BASKET

- Sweet corn should be picked when the kernels are plump and full. To test for ripeness, pull a husk about a third of the way down the ear and press your thumbnail into a kernel. If milk spurts out readily, the ear is ripe. Note that kernels that have no milk are past their prime and kernels that spurt a nonmilky, clear liquid are immature.
- In some varieties, the appearance of corn silk is another indicator of ripeness. If the silk is brown and slightly dry, the ear is ripe. At this stage, the top of the cob should be rounded and blunt rather than pointed.
- Remove a cob from its stalk by giving it a sharp, downward twist.
- The best time to pick corn is very early in the morning because the sugar level in the kernels is at its highest. As the day progresses and becomes warmer, the sugar is converted to starch. So, if you pick your corn in the afternoon, it won't be as sweet as ears picked in the morning. Unless you're having corn for breakfast, hold the ears in the refrigerator until lunch or dinner.

- A preharvest note: There's a critical three-week period that begins about five days before silking and ends in harvest. During this time, corn can take about one-third inch of water each day. If temperatures are unusually high and humidity is low, corn can take one-half inch of water per day. Remember that in just four days, lack of moisture during this period can reduce your yield by more than half.

INDOOR STORAGE

- The minute corn is picked, the sugar in its kernels begins to turn to starch, and the quality starts to deteriorate. For best results, corn should be cooked, canned, or frozen immediately.
- If you must hold corn, refrigerate it unhusked. Several hours is okay, overnight is less okay, but in a day or more, much of the freshly picked sweetness will be lost from most varieties.
- Never, ever store corn at room temperature.

Keeping Corn

- To help retain texture and flavor when freezing corn kernels, blanch them while they're still on the cob.
- When canning creamed corn, always use pint-sized jars. When canned in quarts, creamed corn tends to darken.

CULINARY TECHNIQUES

Two Ways to Remove Corn Silk

1. Pull down the husks and remove the silk by rubbing it off under running water.
2. Pull down the husks and scrape away the silk with a dry vegetable brush.

Coaxing Kernels from the Cob

To remove the kernels from their cobs, hold a cob almost vertically; starting at one end, run a sharp knife down to the other end, cutting off kernels as you go. Take care not to cut away any cob.

Weights and Measures

about 2 medium-size ears
= 1 cup of kernels

If you're removing big batches of kernels, a corn cutter and creamer is a handy device to have around. It cuts and creams kernels and easily converts to a whole-kernel cutter.

What Is Corn Milk?

Simply, corn milk is pureed corn. To make it, toss some kernels into a blender or processor and whiz until pureed. The pale yellow cream that results is corn milk. Stir it into sauces and soups as a natural, low-fat thickener, or use it to replace some of the liquid in baking. It freezes well, and its soft, sweet flavor complements tomatoes, peppers, onions, fish, poultry, pork, and most herbs. One-half cup of kernels will yield about one-third cup of corn milk.

tip

For flavor, texture, and color, toss a handful of lightly blanched corn kernels into pasta salads, mixed green salads, hot or cold soups, dips, sandwich fillings, bread dough, stews, or casseroles.

OK, NEXT YEAR

- Xtra-Sweet, Sugar Extender, Early Xtra-Sweet, Illini Xtra-Sweet, and Summer Sweet are Everlasting Heritage varieties that, if refrigerated, will keep their sweet flavor for several days to two weeks longer than many varieties.
- Most hybrid sweet corn varieties should be isolated to prevent cross-pollination. Barrier plants like sunflowers work well.
- Tips for an early harvest include planting on a southern slope in well-drained soil, not planting too deep, and using black plastic mulch. In fact, some gardeners say that corn planted under plastic matures 10 to 14 days earlier.
- Help avoid corn borers by planting after the spring ground has completely warmed.
- Many gardeners prefer open-pollinated corn to hybrid because they feel the flavor is superior. Try Country Gentleman, Stowell's Evergreen, and Golden Bantam.
- Planning to can or freeze? Choose Golden Cross Bantam, Iochief, and Illini Chief.
- Stretch your corn harvest by putting in several varieties that will mature a week apart or make a weekly planting of one variety.
- Yes, corn can actually be planted in containers. For good pollination, plant the corn in groups. Varieties to try include Golden Midget and Midget Hybrid. Plants are about three feet tall and mature ears are about four inches long.
- If you're looking for a table corn that can also be ground into cornmeal, plant Black Mexican (white kernels at table stage, purple-blue when dried and ground), Black Aztec (white at table stage, black when dried), or Midnight Snack (yellow at table stage, blue-black when dried).
- Hickory King is a favorite variety for making grits and hominy.

Corn Chowder with Five Vegetables

makes about 5 cups

1 tablespoon corn oil
2 medium-size onions, chopped
3 stalks celery, diagonally sliced
¼ cup minced celery leaves
1 medium-size carrot, diced
2 medium-size potatoes, diced
1 sprig thyme or 1 teaspoon dried thyme
1 tablespoon minced fresh summer savory
 or 1 teaspoon dried savory
3 bay leaves
2 to 3 cups chicken stock
4½ cups corn kernels
2 to 2½ cups milk
½ teaspoon freshly ground white pepper, or to taste
 fresh thyme leaves for garnish (optional)

In a 3- or 4-quart saucepan, heat oil over low heat. Add onions, celery stalks and leaves, and carrots. Sauté until soft, about 10 minutes, stirring frequently. Add potatoes, thyme, savory, bay leaves, and enough stock to cover vegetables. Bring to a boil. Reduce heat, partially cover, and simmer for 20 to 25 minutes, or until vegetables are tender. Discard thyme sprig and bay leaves.

Puree 1½ cups of the corn kernels in a food processor or blender. Add pureed corn and remaining whole kernels to simmering vegetables. Cook over low heat for about 10 minutes, or until corn is tender. Add about 2 cups of the milk and simmer for about 5 minutes, or until heated through (don't let mixture boil). Add more milk, if necessary, so that mixture is medium thick. Season with white pepper. Garnish with thyme leaves, if desired.

Marinated Baby Corn

4 servings

Baby corn can be harvested from any sweet corn plant, preferably a multi-ear producer. Harvest when the silks just begin to peek out from the husks.

Marinated Baby Corn

> Indian Cornmeal
>
> The kernels of ornamental (Indian) corn can be roasted, then ground into meal, and made into corn bread.

  3 cups water
¼ cup olive oil
¼ cup balsamic vinegar
½ teaspoon honey
  4 slices onion
  4 thin slices lemon
  2 cloves garlic
  2 bay leaves
  1 teaspoon dried basil
¼ teaspoon dried marjoram
12 ears of baby corn

In a medium-size saucepan, combine water, oil, vinegar, honey, onions, and lemon. Gather together garlic, bay leaves, basil, and marjoram in a piece of cheesecloth, tie, and add to saucepan. Bring to a boil. Remove from heat and let stand for 15 minutes. Remove cheesecloth bag. Bring to a simmer. Add corn and simmer for 6 to 8 minutes, or until tender. Remove corn with a slotted spoon and place in a casserole dish. Pour marinade over corn, cover, and refrigerate for at least 2 hours, or overnight. Drain off marinade before serving.

X-Rated Corn

Corn smut may not be what you think. Many gardeners view the ultra-ugly fungus as something that must be eliminated immediately. However, in Mexico, corn smut or *cuitlacoche* (kweet-lah-KOE-chay) is eaten with gusto in soups, stews, sauces, sautés, and as fillings for tortillas.

Soft Corn Tortillas

makes 16 tortillas

Serve with dips and salsas or fill with beans and vegetables.

¼ cup masa harina*
¼ cup unbleached white flour
¼ teaspoon ground turmeric
1 egg
½ cup corn milk (page 49)
½ cup buttermilk
1 tablespoon minced fresh chives
2 teaspoons oil

In a medium-size bowl, combine masa harina, flour, and turmeric.

In another bowl, combine egg, corn milk, buttermilk, and chives. Add wet mixture to dry and combine.

Heat a nonstick crepe pan and brush with some oil. Add about 2 tablespoons of batter to the pan and swirl pan until batter forms a round crepe. Cook for several minutes on each side, or until crepe is dotted with reddish brown. Repeat with remaining batter.

*Masa harina is a finely ground cornmeal and is available at many supermarkets and specialty food stores.

Corn and Spinach Strudel

6 to 8 servings

1 cup part-skim ricotta cheese
1½ cups cooked corn kernels
1 cup cooked chopped spinach, drained well
1 egg, beaten
2 tablespoons grated Parmesan cheese
6 phyllo dough sheets
2 tablespoons butter, melted
⅓ cup whole grain bread crumbs

Preheat oven to 375°F.

In a large mixing bowl, combine ricotta cheese, corn, spinach, egg, and Parmesan. Mix well and set aside.

Corn and Spinach Strudel

Place 2 phyllo sheets on waxed paper on a damp towel. Brush lightly with melted butter. Sprinkle with half of the bread crumbs. Repeat this procedure with 2 more of the sheets, butter, and bread crumbs. Add the last 2 sheets and brush with butter. With long end of the dough parallel to the table, spread cheese mixture over phyllo dough, leaving an inch on all sides. With the help of the damp towel, fold sides over mixture so that it covers ½ inch on each side. Brush edges lightly with water so that it does not unfold.

Again with the help of the towel, roll dough away from you onto a baking sheet sprayed with vegetable spray. Bake for about 30 minutes, or until lightly browned. Serve warm.

Don't Throw Those Husks Away!

Foods like rice, polenta, and fish are delicious when steamed in packages made of fresh corn husks. Simply soak the husks in water for about 15 minutes, then place the food on the husk and fold and wrap to form a sealed package. Then place into a steamer, seam-side down. A fish fillet, for example, will take 15 to 20 minutes to cook. Herbs, citrus, and other aromatics may be added to the package.

tip

Make breakfast more deli-
cious and healthful by adding
lightly blanched corn kernels
to pancake batter, waffle batter, hot cereals, omelets, and
scrambled eggs. Or sauté
them with strips of green and
sweet red peppers and then
add to omelets.

Buttermilk Corn Bread

6 to 8 servings

½ cup whole wheat flour
½ cup unbleached white flour
2 teaspoons baking powder
½ teaspoon baking soda
1 cup cornmeal
1¼ cups buttermilk
1 egg, slightly beaten
3 tablespoons plus 1 teaspoon corn oil, divided
2 tablespoons honey
1 cup fresh or thawed frozen corn kernels

In a large bowl, sift together whole wheat flour, white flour, baking powder, and baking soda. Stir in cornmeal.

In a small bowl, combine buttermilk, egg, 3 tablespoons of the oil, and honey. Add liquid mixture to dry mixture, along with corn kernels, and stir batter until it is just combined.

Preheat oven to 425°F.

Coat an 8-inch-square pan or a 9-inch pie plate with remaining oil. Place in oven for 5 minutes, or until hot. Pour in batter, smoothing top with a spatula. Bake for 20 to 25 minutes, or until top is golden and bread tests done. Let cool in pan on a rack for 5 minutes. Cut into squares or wedges to serve.

Corn Nuts

makes 1 cup

Add to nut mixes, toss into salads, or use to garnish soups.

1 cup cooked hominy
1 teaspoon corn oil

Dry hominy thoroughly on paper towels. Toss with oil. Spread out on baking sheet. Bake in a preheated 500°F oven until lightly toasted.

Variation: While toasted corn nuts are still warm, toss with a pinch each of paprika, ground cumin, dried oregano, chili powder, or any herb combination you like.

Flavored Butters for Corn

Enjoy these accompaniments with grilled, roasted, or steamed ears.

Paprika and Lime Butter:
1 tablespoon lime juice
1 teaspoon paprika
¼ cup butter, softened

   Add lime juice and paprika to butter and mix well.

Herb Butter:
2 tablespoons minced fresh parsley
2 tablespoons minced fresh chives
2 teaspoons minced scallions
½ teaspoon lemon juice
¼ cup butter, softened

   Add parsley, chives, scallions, and lemon juice to butter and mix well.

Italian Butter:
2 tablespoons minced fresh basil
¼ teaspoon minced fresh oregano
1 tablespoon grated Parmesan cheese
¼ cup butter, softened

   Add basil, oregano, and cheese to butter and mix well.

What's Hominy?

Dried kernels of corn are soaked in a weak lime solution until the skins come off. Then, the skinless kernels are cooked in water until they soften and enlarge.

Hominy is enjoyed much the same way that we enjoy corn. It can be eaten as a simple side dish or made into an elaborate Mexican/Indian stew called *pozole* (poe-ZOE-lay).

Popcorn

Burpee Peppy and Strawberry are two popular popcorn varieties. Generally, ears are slim and two to four inches long. To harvest, leave mature ears on unwatered stalks until the first hard frost. Twist the ears off the stalks and pull off the husks. Then cut out any insect damage or mold. Place the ears in a ventilated carton or basket in a cellar or garage and let them cure for about a month. Test for dryness by trying to pop a few kernels. If they're dry enough, they'll pop. To store popcorn, twist the kernels off the cobs and store in covered glass jars in a cool place.

   Use popped corn as a garnish in soups or salads. Or grind popcorn finely and sprinkle on cakes and cookies in place of powdered sugar.

tip

The Easiest Creamed Corn

Blanch husked ears for about 5 minutes. Then use a serrated knife to slit each row of kernels in half. Remove the kernels from the cob and freeze or heat through and serve.

Baked Corn Custard with Pecans

6 servings

2 cups milk
1 teaspoon grated lime peel
1 tablespoon minced ginger root
3 eggs, room temperature
¼ cup honey, warmed
3 tablespoons ground pecans
½ teaspoon vanilla extract
½ cup fresh or thawed frozen corn kernels
    ground nutmeg to sprinkle

In a heavy, medium-size saucepan, combine milk, lime peel, and ginger. Bring just to a boil. Remove from heat, cover, and steep for 20 minutes. Pour through a fine strainer, pressing on lime peel and ginger with the back of a spoon.

In a large bowl, whisk eggs lightly until smooth but not frothy. Gently whisk in honey until just combined. Whisk in milk in a slow stream. Stir in pecans, vanilla, and corn.

Preheat oven to 325°F.

Butter 6 individual custard cups and set on a wire rack in a roaster pan. Pour custard mixture into cups, skim off foam from tops, and sprinkle with nutmeg. Pour enough very hot water into pan to come halfway up sides of cups. Bake for 30 to 45 minutes, or until a thin knife inserted halfway between the center and the edge of each custard comes out clean. Remove immediately from water bath and let cool. Serve at room temperature or chill.

Corn and Sweet Pepper Custard

6 servings

Serve with a green salad and a mixed vegetable soup.

2 tablespoons thinly sliced green peppers
2 tablespoons thinly sliced sweet red peppers
1 tablespoon butter
1 small onion, minced
1½ cups cooked corn kernels
⅔ cup grated sharp cheddar cheese
1 plum tomato, seeded, quartered, and dried on paper towels

Corn and Sweet Pepper Custard

3 eggs
⅔ cup milk
⅓ cup corn milk (page 49)
1 tablespoon unbleached white flour
⅛ teaspoon freshly ground white pepper
⅛ teaspoon cayenne pepper

Steam green and red pepper slices for 3 minutes. Drain and pat dry on paper towels. Set aside.

In a small saucepan, melt butter over low heat. Add onions and sauté for 4 minutes, or until tender. Add corn and sauté for 1 minute.

Preheat oven to 350°F.

Lightly coat an 8-inch shallow casserole with vegetable spray. Spoon half of the corn mixture into casserole. Arrange half of the pepper slices on top of this, then sprinkle with half of the cheese. Repeat with remaining corn mixture, pepper slices, and cheese. Top with tomato quarters.

In a medium bowl, beat eggs. Add milk, corn milk, flour, white pepper, and cayenne, and beat thoroughly. Slowly pour into casserole. Bake for 40 to 45 minutes, or until a knife inserted into the center comes out clean and top is lightly browned. Let cool on a rack for 20 minutes. Cut into wedges to serve.

CHAPTER 6

CUCUMBERS

The expression "cool as a cucumber" is no idle comparison. In fact, the internal temperature of a cuke can be as much as 20 degrees cooler than the outside air on a hot day. This must be why many hot-weather cuisines accompany their spicy dishes with cucumbers.

If you have a favorite hot chili recipe, you can make your own cucumber refresher to go with it. Slice three medium cukes and toss them into a salad bowl. Then whisk together one teaspoon each of freshly ground cumin and coriander seeds, a clove of minced garlic, three tablespoons of apple cider vinegar, one tablespoon of fruity olive oil, and a pinch each of dried mustard and oregano. Toss with the cukes, chill, and serve.

INTO THE BASKET

- Cucumbers should be picked when they are no longer than seven inches, except for the longer-growing varieties like burpless or Chinese cucumbers. They can become bitter if left to grow longer.
- Cut cukes from the stem gently, using a sharp knife or kitchen shears.
- Picking cucumbers promptly and before they mature will help insure a high yield.

INDOOR STORAGE

Cucumbers sealed in plastic bags and stored in the crisper drawer of the refrigerator will last for about ten days. Cucumbers don't freeze well because they lose too much texture and flavor.

CULINARY TECHNIQUES

Peeling—Decorative and Otherwise

Peel cukes if the skin is tough and bitter, using a swivel-blade vegetable peeler or a sharp paring knife.

Decorative peeling can be done in several ways. The most popular is to score the skin by making vertical top-to-bottom sweeps with a sharp-tined fork. You can also score the skin in vertical stripes, using a vegetable scorer or canelle knife (the same tool you use for removing citrus peel strips for beverages). If you prefer wide vertical stripes or swirls, make them with a swivel-blade vegetable peeler or a sharp paring knife.

Cuke Garnishes

- Cut a lemon in half lengthwise and set each half on a surface, cut-side down. Then make vertical slits in the halves that don't go quite all the way through. Tuck a thin cucumber slice into each slit and use to garnish platters.
- Using scored slices, make a cut in each that goes from the middle to the edge. Hold the slice in both hands, one hand on either side of the slit. Then twist the slice to form an S, and use it to garnish fish or chicken.

▰▰ OK, NEXT YEAR ▰▰

- Eversweet, Saticoy, Country Fair, Sweet Slice, and Spartan Salad are varieties that are guaranteed not to be bitter. They're also resistant to cucumber beetles.
- Thin-skinned varieties that are easy to digest include Burpless, Green Knight, Country Fair, Tasty Green, Burpless Hybrid, and oriental varieties like Suyo and Japanese Climbing.
- Spacemaster, Bush Whopper, Patio Pik, and Burpless Bush Hybrid are bush cucumbers with high yields for small gardens.
- Marketmore 70 is resistant to cucumber mosaic virus and scab; Marketmore 76 is resistant to cucumber mosaic virus, scab, downy mildew, and powdery mildew; Marketmore 86 resists all of the above plus striped cucumber beetles.
- Good slicers, which have smooth skins, include Early Triumph, Sweet Slice, Dasher II, Victory, and Sweet Success.
- Good picklers, which have lumpy skins, include Carolina, Salvo (white spined), Saladin (black spined), Ohio MR17, SMR-18, and Explorer.
- Seedless varieties to try are Country Fair and Sweet Success.
- Lemon cukes are round and yellow and delicious pickled or in salads.
- Good climbers include Sanjakukiuri, China Hybrid, Armenian, China Long, Green Ice, Japanese Climbing, Kyoto Three Feet, and Sooyoo.

Cucumber Melons

Armenian (or Beit Alpha) cucumbers look and taste like cukes, but actually, they're melons. They're popular in Middle-Eastern cuisines and are delicious braised, stuffed, or stewed, or in salads. Varieties to try include Amira and Armenian.

Cucumber Cups with Salmon Tartare

makes about 24 appetizers

½ pound salmon
  juice of 3 limes
1 jalapeño pepper, halved lengthwise, seeded, and minced
  pinch of dried marjoram
1 tablespoon lemon juice
2 large cucumbers

Mince salmon with a large knife and toss with lime juice in a nonmetallic dish. Cover with plastic wrap, refrigerate, and allow fish to marinate for at least 4 hours, preferably overnight.

When you're ready to serve, drain salmon and combine with jalapeño, marjoram, and lemon juice. Then set aside while you prepare cucumber cups.

Score cukes lengthwise with a sharp-tined fork, canelle knife, or vegetable scorer. Slice off ends and continue to slice cukes into ½-inch-thick slices. Then hollow out with a melon baller, leaving enough bottom and sides to hold salmon. Fill cups and serve immediately.

Quick Cuke Appetizers

Cucumber *Raita*

4 to 6 servings

1½ pounds cucumbers
½ teaspoon cumin seeds
½ teaspoon coriander seeds
⅛ teaspoon freshly ground white pepper
2 cups plain yogurt, drained for 10 minutes
3 scallions (white part plus 1 inch of green part),
    finely minced
1 medium-size tomato, pulp and seeds removed,
    cut into thin strips
1 green chili, seeded and thinly sliced
1 tablespoon minced fresh coriander (cilantro)
    or fresh parsley for garnish

Cut cucumbers in half lengthwise, then into quarters. If seeds are large, remove them. Shred cucumbers on medium side of a hand grater and place in a sieve to drain for 30 minutes.

Toss cumin seeds into a small skillet and roast over low heat, stirring frequently, until seeds brown, about 5 minutes. Cool, then crush seeds. Roast coriander seeds until light brown, about 3 minutes, cool, and then crush. (Roasting helps bring out flavor of seeds.)

Squeeze cucumbers with your hands, then drain them on paper towels.

In a medium-size bowl, combine cucumbers, cumin, coriander, white pepper, yogurt, scallions, tomatoes, and chili, and stir gently. Chill or serve immediately.

Stir before serving and garnish with coriander or parsley.

Low-Cal Cukes

One large cucumber contains about 25 calories.

Cucumber Soup with Pistou

4 servings

Soup:
1 tablespoon olive oil
1 leek (white part plus 1 inch of green), chopped
1 stalk celery with leaves, chopped
1 pound cucumbers, peeled, halved, seeded, and chopped
2 teaspoons lemon juice
4 cups chicken stock

Pistou:
2 cloves garlic, finely minced
¼ cup minced fresh basil
4 teaspoons finely chopped walnuts
2 teaspoons Parmesan cheese
4 teaspoons olive oil
½ medium-size tomato, peeled, seeded, and chopped

To prepare the soup: In a medium-size saucepan, heat oil over low heat. Add leeks and celery and cook until vegetables are soft, about 10 minutes, stirring occasionally. Add cucumbers, lemon juice, and stock. Bring to a boil over medium heat. Reduce heat to low and simmer for 20 minutes, or until cucumbers are tender. Cool slightly.

To prepare the pistou: With a mortar and pestle, mash together garlic, basil, and walnuts to a paste. (You can also use a bowl with a wooden spoon.) Work in a little cheese and oil and one-third of the tomato. Keep adding cheese, oil, and tomato. The mixture will not be a true emulsion but a barely fluid paste.

Transfer cucumber mixture to a food processor or blender and puree, in batches, until smooth. Ladle soup into serving bowl. Pass the pistou. Allow 1 tablespoon of pistou per serving to be placed in the center of bowl, then swirled into soup.

Oil of Cucumber

Cucumber-seed oil is used in some of the cuisines of Africa for flavoring and adding body to soups, stews, and purees.

Cucumbers with Sushi Rice

4 servings

    1 cup short-grain, Japanese-style rice
1¼ cups water
    1 tablespoon rice vinegar
    1 tablespoon mirin*
    1 cucumber, cut into julienne strips
    2 tablespoons toasted sesame seeds
    2 scallions, finely minced
      sesame oil to sprinkle

Rinse rice, then combine in a medium-size saucepan with water and let stand for 30 minutes. Then bring to a boil, reduce heat immediately, and simmer, stirring frequently, until all water has been absorbed. Remove rice from heat and stir in rice vinegar, mirin, cucumbers, and sesame seeds.

Serve warm or at room temperature with scallions and sesame oil to sprinkle.

*Mirin is a sweet rice vinegar and is available at specialty food stores, oriental markets, and many supermarkets.

tip

Freezer Pickles

Slice pickling cucumbers thinly into rounds and layer them in quart freezer containers with sliced onions. Toss in fresh herbs such as dill, thyme, or basil, using about 4 sprigs per quart. If you have very fresh garlic, add a clove to each quart. Mustard seeds, cumin seeds, coriander seeds, and allspice berries work well, too. Cover the pickles with vinegar and honey, using about 4 parts vinegar to 1 part honey. If the liquid doesn't cover the pickles, add more vinegar. Cover the containers and freeze for up to 3 months in the freezer or 1 week in the refrigerator. To defrost the pickles, leave them overnight in the refrigerator.

Crushed Cucumbers with Chicken

4 servings

Crushing helps the cukes absorb the surrounding flavors.

    1 scallion, cut into 2-inch pieces and crushed
    1 slice (¼ inch thick) ginger root
  ⅛ teaspoon Szechuan peppercorns
    2 whole boneless chicken breasts (about 1½ pounds)
  ¼ cup rice vinegar
  ¼ cup soy sauce
  ¼ cup Dijon mustard
    2 tablespoons honey
  ¼ teaspoon sesame oil
    2 large cucumbers, peeled, cut in half lengthwise, and seeded

In a medium-size skillet, combine scallions, ginger, pepper-corns, and enough water to cover chicken. Bring to a boil. Add chicken, reduce heat to low, cover, and simmer gently for about 10 minutes, or until chicken is tender. Remove from heat and let cool.

In a small bowl, whisk together vinegar, soy sauce, mustard, honey, and oil until thoroughly combined.

Cut each cucumber half in half crosswise. Place 1 portion of cucumber under a small cast-iron skillet wrapped with aluminum foil. (Any heavy item such as a plate or flat side of a cleaver may be used.) Press skillet down on cucumber so that cucumber breaks apart but remains intact. Place cucumber carefully on an individual serving dish. Repeat with remaining cucumber portions, placing 2 crushed cucumber portions on each plate.

Remove chicken breasts from water and drain well. Diago-nally cut into thin slices and arrange them on top of cucumbers in a circular design. Pour a ladleful of sauce over each cucumber-chicken arrangement and serve immediately.

Cold Poached Haddock with Cucumber and Dill

4 servings

2 cucumbers, peeled, halved, seeded, and finely diced
 juice of 1 lemon
2 teaspoons finely chopped fresh dill
2 pounds haddock fillets, ½ to 1 inch thick

In a medium-size bowl, gently combine cucumbers, lemon juice, and dill. Refrigerate, covered, for about 30 minutes. You'll have about 2 cups.

Choose a saucepan large enough to hold haddock fillets in a single layer. Fill it with enough water or stock to cover fillets and bring water to a boil. Add fillets to pan, and lower heat to a gentle simmer. Cook fillets for about 5 minutes, or until fish flakes easily with a fork. Remove fillets with a slotted spoon and let them cool.

Serve fish cold or at room temperature, topped with cucumber mixture.

Ideas for Cucumber Salads

- cucumber chunks, steamed shrimp, avocado chunks, lime juice, and olive oil
- cucumber slices, shred-ded cooked chicken, sweet red peppers, Dijon mustard, olive oil, and lemon juice
- cucumber spears and blanched leeks with a sauce of Dijon mustard and plain yogurt
- cucumber chunks, fiddle-head ferns, and ruby let-tuce with freshly grated orange peel and apple ci-der vinegar
- cucumber slices, blanched snow peas, and slivered dried tomatoes with freshly grated Par-mesan cheese
- thin cucumber slices, nasturtium blossoms, and dill sprigs, served over lettuce and sprinkled with apple cider vinegar
- cucumber slices, blueber-ries, purple onion slices, watercress, mace, and rice vinegar
- cucumber chunks, shiitake mushrooms, wa-ter chestnuts, ginger, gar-lic, lemon juice, and toasted sesame seeds
- cucumber slices, cooked crabmeat, minced onions, curry powder, and plain yogurt

And the Winner Is . . .

The longest cucumber ever grown measured 49 inches and was grown in Buffalo, Missouri.

Dilled Cucumber Puree

makes about 1 cup

¼ cup chicken or vegetable stock
1 pound cucumbers, peeled, halved, seeded,
   and coarsely chopped
2 tablespoons mayonnaise or plain yogurt
1 tablespoon finely minced fresh dill

 Bring stock to a boil in a small saucepan and add cucumbers. Reduce heat to low, cover, and simmer for 20 minutes, or until cucumbers are tender. Let them cool slightly.
 Transfer mixture to a food processor or blender and puree until smooth. Pour into a small bowl, stir in mayonnaise or yogurt, and serve immediately as a side dish with fish, chicken, pork, or pâtés.

Note: The puree may be thinned with skim milk to make a delicious and refreshing salad dressing.

Cucumber and Cantaloupe Ice

makes about 1 quart

1 cup water
⅓ cup honey
3 sprigs mint
1 pound cucumbers, peeled, halved, and seeded
½ medium-size cantaloupe
1½ tablespoons lime juice

 In a small saucepan, combine water, honey, and mint, and bring to a boil. Boil gently for 5 minutes. Remove from heat and let cool. Cover and refrigerate until chilled.
 In a food processor or blender, puree cucumbers until smooth (you should have about 1¼ cups puree). Pour into a medium-size bowl and set aside while you prepare marinade.
 Remove rind and seeds from cantaloupe and cut it into cubes. In a food processor or blender, puree until smooth (you should

Cucumber and Cantaloupe Ice

have about 1 cup puree). Stir in lime juice. Add cucumbers, stir, and chill.

Stir honey syrup into cucumber mixture. Pour into chilled container of an ice cream maker and freeze according to manufacturer's directions. You can also still-freeze the ice. Simply pour mixture into a 9-inch-square pan and cover with foil. Then freeze it until firm, 3 or 4 hours. Break into small pieces and spoon half of the mixture into a chilled food processor bowl. Beat with a metal blade until light and fluffy but not thawed. Repeat with remaining frozen mixture. Serve immediately or return to pan and freeze until firm.

CHAPTER 7

ONIONS

Onions and other members of their large family (which includes garlic, leeks, shallots, and chives) are the most frequently used food flavoring in the world. Onions appear in every cuisine and on every menu in every kitchen.

Onions are recognized as the Kings of Pungency, but actually their flavors vary depending on how they're prepared. For instance, long roasting makes onions sweet; stewing makes them mellow; and grated raw onions have a verve all their own.

Garlic can change personalities, too. For example, minced fresh in a vinaigrette, garlic is sharp and strong. But roasted, it's soft flavored and nutty.

INTO THE BASKET

- Harvest scallions when they are no taller than ten inches. Harvesting scallions also serves as a thinning process, giving other onions a chance to mature to larger bulbs.
- Pickling, pearl, or baby onions can be harvested when the bulbs are an inch or less in diameter. Gently push the soil aside to check size.
- Mature onions can be left in the ground until their tops fall over. If some tops remain erect at the end of the growing season, bend them over with your foot or a rake. Then leave the bulbs in the ground for about a week before curing and storing them. Never leave onions in the ground for the winter because the ground is too wet and can cause the bulbs to rot.

INDOOR STORAGE

Short-term Storage

- Scallions age quickly and should be wrapped in plastic and kept in the crisper drawer in the refrigerator. They will keep there for up to ten days.
- Whole onions should not be refrigerated. Instead, keep them in a cool, well-ventilated place, like a root cellar, until you are ready to use them.
- Store cut onions, wrapped in plastic, in the refrigerator.

Long-term Storage

To prepare onions for long-term storage, brush off the dirt and leave the tops and skins intact (the skins help prevent sprouting). Then cure by leaving them in a shady, airy, dry area for about a week or until the necks dry completely and the roots look wiry.

CULINARY TECHNIQUES

Easy Peeling

Drop onions into boiling water for about two minutes. Then plunge them into cold water, remove, and peel. This trick is especially useful when peeling pounds of onions for pickling.

Easy Chopping

Using a sharp chef's knife, cut off the stem end (leave the root end) and peel. Lay the onion on its side and make parallel vertical cuts through the onion, leaving it attached at the stem. Next, make several horizontal cuts, again leaving the root intact. Then, holding the point of the knife down with your hand, chop until you have the size you want.

Amazing Onion Ideas

Here are suggestions for onion appetizers, salads, and side dishes:

- Cut onions into eighths and simmer in stock for about 10 minutes. Transfer onions to a bowl, sprinkle with freshly grated pepper, a bit of olive oil, white wine vinegar, lemon juice, and thyme. Cover and chill. Serve with red leaf lettuce.
- In a medium-size saucepan, combine slices of sweet onion and chopped chives with a bit of apple cider vinegar, a bit of honey, freshly grated nutmeg, and some paprika. Bring the mixture to a boil, then simmer until thick, about 20 minutes. Serve warm with crusty French bread or chill and serve with plain yogurt.
- Simmer tiny onions (or quartered large ones) in tomato sauce, minced garlic, and oregano for about an hour, or until the sauce is greatly reduced. Add a splash of balsamic vinegar and chill. Serve with crisp, thin toast, as a condiment for beef or chicken, or with broccoli or other vegetables.
- Sauté sliced onions in sweet butter with pine nuts and raisins. Toss on poached swordfish or grilled beef tenderloin.

OK, NEXT YEAR

- Onions grown from seed store better than those grown from sets. Onions that are especially good for storing are Autumn Spice and Spartan Sleeper.
- Seed varieties that produce good scallions include Evergreen Bunching, Beltsville Bunching, and Southport Bunching.
- Bermuda and Spanish onions don't store well. Instead, try Yellow Globe, Yellow Globe Danvers, Ebenezer, Wethersfield, Southport Red Globe, Fiesta, Spartan Sleeper, Sweet Sandwich, Northern Oak, and Enterprise.
- When storing onion sets for planting next year, you can discourage bolting by keeping the size to under ¾ inch. It's also important to store sets at 30° to 35°F.
- Avoid split bulbs by planting in well-drained soil.
- Granex, Sweet Sandwich, Grano, Sweet Winter, Spanish, Crystal Wax, Balbosa, Vidalia, Walla Walla, and Valencia are extra-sweet varieties.
- For giant-sized onions, try Utah, Yellow Sweet Spanish, and White Sweet Spanish.

tip

Two Ways to Caramelize Onions

This savory technique adds flavor and color to soups, sauces, and stews.

- Bake quartered onions in about an inch of stock in a 350°F oven for an hour and a quarter or until a deep reddish brown. Use as is or puree.
- Sauté chopped onions in butter (apologies to dieters, but stock won't work) for about 25 minutes or until a deep reddish brown. Use as is or puree.

Ditalini with Four Onions

6 servings

1 cup baby onions, steamed until tender
½ red onion, thinly sliced and separated into rings
3 scallions, minced
1 cup sliced mushrooms
1 carrot, cut into julienne strips
1 red pepper, diced
2 cups cooked ditalini (elbow macaroni may be substituted)
1 teaspoon peanut oil
¼ cup white wine vinegar
1 teaspoon minced ginger root
½ teaspoon fennel seeds, crushed
¼ teaspoon ground turmeric
2 shallots, quartered

In a large bowl, combine baby onions, red onions, scallions, mushrooms, carrots, peppers, and ditalini. Set aside.

In a blender, combine oil, vinegar, ginger, fennel, turmeric, and shallots, and whiz until smooth. Pour over ditalini mixture and toss well before serving.

Onions with Eggplant, Orzo, and Lamb

tip

Making Flavored Vinegar

Heat 1 quart of rice vinegar or white wine vinegar, but don't boil. Then add about ½ cup of chopped onions, 2 peeled cloves of garlic, 1 bay leaf, and 1 peeled shallot to a glass bottle. Pour in the vinegar and seal. Let steep for 2 weeks before straining and using in salads or marinades.

4 or 5 servings

3 tablespoons plus 1 teaspoon olive oil, divided
1 small eggplant, cut into 1-inch cubes
1 pound small white onions
1 pound lean boneless lamb, cut into 1-inch cubes
2 cloves garlic, minced
1 tablespoon tomato paste
⅛ teaspoon dried oregano
⅛ teaspoon dried thyme
   dash of black pepper
1 cup beef stock
   bouquet garni—3 sprigs parsley, 1 sprig thyme,
      and 1 bay leaf, gathered together in a piece of
      cheesecloth and tied with string
1 cup orzo pasta
¼ cup minced onions
1 tomato, peeled, seeded, and chopped
1 tablespoon minced fresh parsley

Heat 2 tablespoons of the oil in a medium-size skillet. Add eggplant and sauté, turning and tossing until browned. Remove with a slotted spoon and drain on paper towels. Add 1 tablespoon of the oil and white onions and sauté for 5 minutes, or until lightly browned. Remove and set aside. Add lamb in batches and brown on all sides. Remove and place in a medium-size casserole.

To the skillet, add garlic, tomato paste, oregano, thyme, pepper, and stock. Bring to a boil over high heat, scraping brown particles clinging to bottom and sides of pan. Pour over lamb in casserole and add bouquet garni and white onions. Bake, covered, at 325°F for 1½ hours, or until lamb is tender. Add eggplant halfway through the cooking time.

Meanwhile, cook orzo in boiling water until tender. In a medium-size skillet, cook minced onions in remaining oil until soft. Add tomatoes and cook for 1 minute. Stir in drained orzo and parsley.

To serve, spoon lamb mixture into center of a serving dish. Surround with orzo.

tip

Onion Puree for Reduced-Salt Diets

Add zip to sauces, soups, and stews with onion puree. To prepare, chop onions and toss into a saucepan with enough stock to cover. Add a bouquet garni consisting of bay and peppercorns, and simmer until the onions are tender, 30 to 40 minutes. Puree the mixture and serve hot with steamed vegetables or as a sauce for meats and poultry.

Barley Pilaf with Onions and Garlic

4 servings

2 tablespoons sesame seeds
2 tablespoons butter
1 large onion, finely chopped
2 cloves garlic, minced
1 cup barley
2½ cups chicken, beef, or vegetable stock
½ teaspoon cumin seeds, crushed
3 allspice berries, crushed

Toast sesame seeds in a heavy skillet over medium heat until golden brown, stirring frequently. Remove from heat and set aside.

Melt butter in same skillet over medium heat. Add onions and garlic and cook until soft, about 5 minutes. Stir in barley and cook, stirring constantly, until grains are coated with butter, 2 or 3 minutes. Add stock, cumin, and allspice. Bring to a boil over high heat. Cover tightly, reduce heat to very low, and simmer for 45 to 55 minutes, or until all liquid has been absorbed.

Stir in sesame seeds and serve.

tip

Making Flavored Oil

Add chopped onions and/or peeled garlic and shallots to a glass jar and cover with fruity olive oil. Store in the refrigerator, using the oil for sautéing and salads and the onions, garlic, and shallots the same ways you would use them if freshly peeled.

Onion Tart with Porcini Mushrooms

10 servings

¼ cup dried porcini mushrooms
½ cup sweet butter, softened
1 cup whole wheat pastry flour
1½ tablespoons grated Parmesan cheese
4 or 5 tablespoons milk
2 large onions, thinly sliced
1 cup half-and-half or milk
3 eggs
   dash of freshly grated nutmeg
   dash of freshly ground pepper
3 scallions, minced (about ¼ cup)

In a small bowl, pour enough water over mushrooms to cover and let soak for about 20 minutes. (You may need to weight them down with a cup.) When soft, drain and mince, reserving both mushrooms and soaking liquid.

Preheat oven to 350°F.

In a medium-size bowl, cut butter into flour and cheese, using a pastry blender or a large fork. When butter is size of large toast crumbs, add milk, tablespoon by tablespoon, until dough is a well-combined, smooth ball. Press into a 10-inch tart pan with removable bottom and freeze for 10 minutes.

Remove crust from freezer and prick with a fork. Bake crust blind (unfilled) for about 20 minutes. While baking, prepare filling.

In a medium-size skillet, combine reserved mushroom soaking liquid and onions and sauté until liquid has disappeared. Remove from heat and arrange onions in bottom of baked crust.

In a medium-size bowl, combine half-and-half or milk, eggs, nutmeg, and pepper. Toss in scallions and minced mushrooms and pour over onions. Bake for about 40 minutes and serve warm.

tip

Freezing Onions

Spread chopped or sliced onions on baking sheets and freeze. Then pack them into containers or bags, and when you're ready, remove as many as you need. If you're planning to store the onions for more than 3 months, blanch them for 2 minutes first. This will preserve their zip.

tip

Loving Leeks

If you like chopped leeks in soups and stews, you'll love them on their own as a first course or salad. Using 8 leeks, slice off the root and most of the green part and rinse well. Slice the leeks in half vertically and lay them in a fry pan with enough stock to cover. Toss in a bay leaf, cover, and let simmer for about 15 minutes. Drain the leeks, arrange them on individual plates, and serve with a sauce of ½ cup plain yogurt and ½ teaspoon Dijon mustard. Garnish with sprigs of rosemary or thyme.

Stuffed Onion Petals

4 servings

 4 large unpeeled onions
½ pound lean ground pork
½ pound ground veal
 1 tablespoon finely chopped celery
 2 tablespoons chopped fresh chives
 2 tablespoons chopped fresh parsley
   dash of cayenne pepper
½ cup plain yogurt, drained for 10 minutes
 1 cup soft whole wheat bread crumbs
 1 cup beef stock

Place onions in a large saucepan. Add water and bring to a boil. Cover, reduce heat, and simmer for about 20 minutes, or until onions feel tender when pierced with the tip of a knife. Drain onions and let cool.

Using a sharp knife, cut off both ends. Make a cut lengthwise through side of each onion to center. Remove and discard outer skin. Then slip off layers of onions one by one until they are too small to be stuffed. Chop onion pieces that won't be stuffed.

In a medium-size skillet, combine chopped onions, pork, and veal. Sauté over medium heat until meat is lightly browned. Add celery and cook for 1 minute. Remove from heat and stir in chives, parsley, cayenne, yogurt, and bread crumbs.

Fill each onion petal with about 2 tablespoons of stuffing. Place in a baking dish. Pour stock around onion petals. Bake at 350°F for 20 to 25 minutes or until lightly browned.

tip

**Two Quick
Ideas for Scallions**

- Brush whole scallions with olive oil and let sit for about 5 minutes. Then grill, turning frequently, until toasty. Serve with grilled meat or poultry.
- Create a scallion butter for corn, grilled fish, grilled tomatoes, and other vegetables: Combine ½ cup softened sweet butter with 1½ tablespoons of finely minced scallions.

Onion Sauce
for Roasted Meats and Poultry

makes about 1½ cups

2 tablespoons butter
1 pound onions, thinly sliced
1 tablespoon honey
2 small cloves garlic, minced
¼ cup red wine vinegar
⅓ cup beef or chicken stock
¼ teaspoon coarsely ground black pepper
¼ teaspoon crushed coriander seeds

Melt butter in a medium-size skillet over low heat. Add onions, cover, and cook until soft, stirring occasionally, for about 10 minutes.

Add honey and garlic and cook, uncovered, for about 5 minutes, or until onions are beginning to turn reddish brown. Transfer to a food processor or blender and puree until smooth. Return to skillet. Blend in vinegar, stock, pepper, and coriander. Bring to a boil, lower heat, and simmer for 1 minute.

If a thinner sauce is desired, add more stock.

Variation: After pureeing onions, add ½ cup dried apricots or raisins or ⅓ cup dried currants.

tip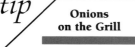

**Onions
on the Grill**

Wrap sweet, unpeeled onions in foil and bury in hot coals for about an hour. Remove foil, peel, and serve as an accompaniment to grilled fish, meat, or poultry.

Grilled Red Onions

4 servings

1 large red onion, cut into ⅓-inch slices (don't separate into rings)
2 teaspoons olive oil

Paint onion slices on both sides with oil and grill or broil for about 4 minutes on each side. Serve with fish, meat, or poultry.

Variation: While slices are still hot, sprinkle with sprigs of thyme or dill.

Pastry Illusions

makes 2½ dozen

The illusion: No one would ever guess that onions are the main ingredient.

Filling:
   4 pounds onions, chopped
   4 pounds plums, chopped
   1 unpeeled lemon, finely chopped
   1 vanilla bean
1½ cups honey

Pastry:
   1 cup whole wheat pastry flour
   1 cup unbleached white flour
   1 cup butter
   ¾ cup cottage cheese
   2 egg whites plus 1 tablespoon water for glazing
      ground cinnamon for sprinkling

To prepare the filling: In a large pot, combine onions, plums, lemon, and vanilla bean, and simmer for 5½ hours, or until mixture is tender and fragrant. Add honey and combine well. Allow mixture to cool slightly before pureeing in a food processor.

To prepare the pastry: Combine whole wheat flour, white flour, butter, and cottage cheese with a pastry blender until mixture becomes a smooth, solid mass. Make 30 walnut-size balls from dough and refrigerate them overnight.

To assemble, flatten a dough ball on a floured counter, using a rolling pin or your hands. The round should be 3 to 3½ inches wide. Place a teaspoon of filling on dough, about ¾ inch from edge of round. Then fold round in half and seal edges by pinching them. Set pastry on a lightly oiled baking sheet and repeat with remaining dough. Glaze with egg white mixture and bake at 375°F for 25 to 30 minutes, or until golden brown. Sprinkle with cinnamon while hot.

Note: You'll have lots of filling left over. It freezes well and can be used as a filling for bar cookies, to line a tart, in quick breads and muffins, or to top a bowl of stewed winter fruit.

Egyptian Onions

Also called tree onions, this variety forms its tiny bulbs on the top of tall stalks. Egyptian onions can also be harvested early and used like scallions. The flavor is stronger than most other types of onions, so use less when chopping into recipes. Egyptian onions are especially delicious when pickled.

CHAPTER 8

PEAS

If an effort to tell one pea from the next has left you confused, here is a quick review. The small, round ones mentioned above are called green peas, English peas, garden peas, or shelled peas.

Flat, edible-podded peas are called oriental peas, snow peas, or sugar peas. Tube-shaped, edible-podded peas are called sugar snap peas.

Black-eyed peas and others of their ilk are called southern table peas, field peas, or cowpeas. Although leguminous and therefore botanically different from green and edible-podded peas, black-eyeds are good and flavorful table company.

INTO THE BASKET

- Peas are ready for picking about three weeks after the blossoms appear. Look for pods that are low on the plant because they'll be ready first.
- Watch the pods closely during ripening, and pick them when they're light green and the peas are not overdeveloped and starchy.
- To pick, hold the stem in one hand while you pinch off the pod with the other hand. Yanking the pods could cause damage to the plant.
- Daily pea picking will encourage high yields.
- If you've let the peas "go by" and they're too starchy to enjoy fresh, leave them on the vine until they're brown, dry, and beginning to split open. Finish off the drying in a low oven or commercial dryer for several hours, then store in a tightly covered container.
- Edible-podded peas should be harvested when the pods are two to three inches long, before the peas start to swell inside the pods.
- Sugar snap peas can be eaten when the pods are still flat, or after the peas are partially developed inside them. The pods remain edible. If the peas have fully developed, shell the sugar snaps and use them like garden peas.

INDOOR STORAGE

Short-term Storage

- Peas should be eaten as soon after picking as possible or their sugars will turn to starch and the taste won't be as wonderful. If you must store peas, don't shell them, but keep them wrapped and refrigerated.
- Edible-podded peas should be stored, unwashed, in sealed plastic bags in the refrigerator, where they'll keep for about ten days.

Long-term Storage

- Freeze peas the same day they're picked, before their natural sugars turn to starch.
- Edible-podded peas become mushy when frozen and are best eaten fresh.

CULINARY TECHNIQUES

Shelling

For maximum flavor, shell peas just before cooking or eating. Some varieties will open for shelling by simply twisting the stem. With others, you'll need to snap off the stem end and zip down the string. And some varieties, when cold, will easily open down the center by pulling the two sides of the pod apart. (The stem doesn't

---

Edible-Podded Peas

Edible-podded peas, such as snow peas and sugar snaps, are wonderful served raw or lightly cooked. First, remove strings, if necessary. Then toss them, raw, into just-served soups as a garnish, or add them the last 15 to 20 seconds of cooking to sautés or stir fries.

If you prefer them blanched, place them in a strainer and pour boiling water over them for about 8 seconds. Or put 1 cup of peas in a dish, cover loosely with crumbled waxed paper, and microwave on full power for 30 seconds.

Edible-podded peas are a great appetizer when served raw or blanched with a dipping sauce or two. Try Dijon mustard, fruited or herbed vinegars, or a mixture of 1-part soy sauce, 1-part stock, and a dash of toasted sesame oil. Edible-podded peas can also be split and topped with ricotta cheese and garnished with a sprig of dill or thyme.

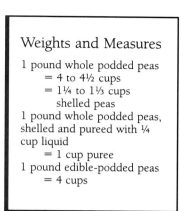

Weights and Measures

1 pound whole podded peas
    = 4 to 4½ cups
    = 1¼ to 1⅓ cups
    shelled peas
1 pound whole podded peas, shelled and pureed with ¼ cup liquid
    = 1 cup puree
1 pound edible-podded peas
    = 4 cups

Edible-Podded Peas

have to be removed.) In any case, to remove the peas from an open pod, run your finger or thumb down the inside of the pod's spine and the peas will snap right out.

Stringing

If your edible-podded peas need stringing, simply snap off the stem end and zip down the string.

OK, NEXT YEAR

- When selecting seeds, choose the wrinkled type, rather than the smooth, because they produce sweeter peas.
- Bush (dwarf) varieties don't need trellising, but have comparatively smaller yields than climbing varieties.
- Popular climbing varieties include Alderman, Green Arrow, Freezonian, Alaska, Sugar Snap, Thomas Laxton, and Wando.
- Burpeeana, Little Marvel, Frosty, and Sparkle are good bush varieties.
- Edible-podded varieties (also called snow or sugar peas) include Oregon Sugar Pod, Mammouth Melting Sugar, Dwarf Grey Sugar, Sugar Snap, Sugar Bon, Sugar Daddy (stringless), and Sugar Ann.
- Varieties recommended for fall planting include Wando, Grenadier, and Perfection Dark Green.
- Succession planting with peas works well if your summers are cool. If they're not, plant a combination of varieties that will mature on successive dates, like Alaska, Blue Bantam, and Wando.
- Novella is a pole variety that supports itself.

Pea Blossoms

Pea blossoms, those delicate white flowers, are edible and make great garnishes for soups and salads.

Quesadillas with Peas and Frizzled Onions

10 servings

⅓ cup chicken stock
¾ cup tomato sauce
½ teaspoon coriander seeds, crushed
½ teaspoon cumin seeds, crushed
1 tablespoon minced fresh oregano
5 flour tortillas (8 inches each)
1 cup coarsely chopped shelled peas
1 ancho chili, soaked and minced
1 cup shredded Monterey Jack cheese, divided
1 small onion, sliced and separated into rings

Preheat oven to 375°F. Lightly oil a 13 × 9-inch baking pan.

In a medium-size saucepan, combine stock, tomato sauce, coriander, cumin, and oregano, and simmer until aromatic, about 10 minutes. Set sauce aside while you prepare the quesadillas.

Using sharp kitchen shears, cut tortillas in half. Prepare filling by combining peas, chili, and ¾ cup of the cheese. Place a mound

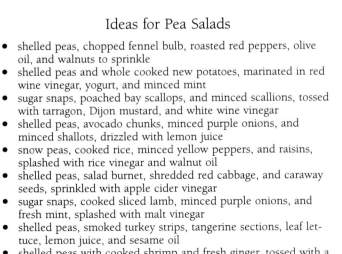

Ideas for Pea Salads

- shelled peas, chopped fennel bulb, roasted red peppers, olive oil, and walnuts to sprinkle
- shelled peas and whole cooked new potatoes, marinated in red wine vinegar, yogurt, and minced mint
- sugar snaps, poached bay scallops, and minced scallions, tossed with tarragon, Dijon mustard, and white wine vinegar
- shelled peas, avocado chunks, minced purple onions, and minced shallots, drizzled with lemon juice
- snow peas, cooked rice, minced yellow peppers, and raisins, splashed with rice vinegar and walnut oil
- shelled peas, salad burnet, shredded red cabbage, and caraway seeds, sprinkled with apple cider vinegar
- sugar snaps, cooked sliced lamb, minced purple onions, and fresh mint, splashed with malt vinegar
- shelled peas, smoked turkey strips, tangerine sections, leaf lettuce, lemon juice, and sesame oil
- shelled peas with cooked shrimp and fresh ginger, tossed with a bit of mayonnaise

of filling on one-half of a halved tortilla and fold the other half over. Set quesadilla into prepared baking pan and continue stuffing tortilla halves. Pour sauce over quesadillas and sprinkle on remaining ¼ cup of cheese. Bake for about 20 minutes, or until cheese has melted and quesadillas are heated through.

While quesadillas are baking, frizzle onions by sautéing over medium-high heat in a dry, nonstick pan. Sprinkle onions over quesadillas before serving.

Steamed Chinese Buns with Peas and Scallions

makes 20 buns

Buns:
½ cup warm water
1 tablespoon honey
1 tablespoon active dry yeast
1 cup whole wheat flour, plus a bit extra for kneading
1 cup unbleached white flour
¾ cup shelled peas
½ cup minced scallions, green part only (about 4 scallions)

Sauce:
¼ cup chicken or beef stock
1 teaspoon soy sauce, or to taste
  splash of sesame oil

To make the buns: In a large bowl, combine water, honey, and yeast. Cover bowl with plastic wrap and let sit for about 10 minutes, or until mixture is bubbly. Then mix in whole wheat flour and white flour until you have a smooth dough. Turn out onto a lightly floured surface and knead for about 6 minutes, adding peas, scallions, and more flour, if necessary. The ball of dough will be smooth and a bit sticky.

Set dough into an oiled bowl, cover with plastic wrap, and let rise in a warm place until doubled in bulk, about 45 minutes.

Pinch off 2-inch rounds from the dough and shape each into a flat-bottomed ball. Steam them in an oiled steamer for about 25 minutes.

To make the sauce: Combine all ingredients in a small bowl. Serve rolls immediately with the sauce for dipping.

Creamy Fish Chowder with Toasted Almonds

4 or 5 servings

    2 tablespoons butter
    1 large leek (white part plus 1 inch of light green), chopped
    1 small onion, chopped
    2 medium-size stalks celery with leaves, chopped
    ½ pound red potatoes (1½ medium size), cut into ½-inch cubes
    2 tablespoons whole wheat flour
    2 cups water or fish stock
        bouquet garni—3 sprigs parsley, 2 sprigs thyme or
            ¼ teaspoon dried thyme, 1 bay leaf, and
            ½ teaspoon mace blades, gathered together
            in a piece of cheesecloth and tied with string
    ½ pound scrod or cod fillets, cut into 1-inch chunks
    1½ cups shelled peas
    1 cup milk
    ½ cup half-and-half
    ⅛ teaspoon freshly grated nutmeg, or to taste
    ⅛ teaspoon freshly ground white pepper, or to taste
    3 tablespoons sliced almonds, toasted
        sweet pea blossoms for garnish

    In a 3-quart saucepan, melt butter over low heat. Add leeks, onions, and celery. Cover pan and cook vegetables until they are soft, about 8 minutes. Add potatoes and cook for 3 minutes, stirring often. Sprinkle with flour and cook, stirring constantly.

Toppings for Cooked Peas

Toss one of these toppings onto just-cooked peas before serving:

- minced roasted red peppers
- chopped nuts
- minced fresh herbs, such as mint, marjoram, or dill
- herb sprigs, such as thyme or chervil
- finely minced shallots or garlic
- sautéed sliced mushrooms
- finely minced water chestnuts or shiitake mushrooms
- toasted sesame seeds or toasted pine nuts

Gradually stir in water or fish stock. Add bouquet garni. Bring to a boil, cover, and simmer until potatoes are tender. Add fish, peas, milk, half-and-half, nutmeg, and pepper. Simmer for 5 to 8 minutes, or until fish is opaque and peas are tender. Discard bouquet garni. Ladle into individual serving bowls. Sprinkle with toasted almonds and garnish with sweet pea blossoms.

Baby Peas

Petit pois, the tiny peas popular in French cooking, are often combined with cooked chopped chestnuts and tarragon or chervil.

Aromatic Rice with Clams

4 servings

1½ cups water
1 cup rice, preferably aromatic or basmati (not quick cooking)
¼ cup grated Parmesan cheese
1 tablespoon minced fresh basil
1 tablespoon minced fresh thyme
1 tablespoon minced fresh lovage or celery leaves
1 cup shelled peas or sugar snap peas
20 to 24 littleneck clams

In a large skillet or paella pan, boil water. Add rice and cook, uncovered, for about 7 minutes. Toss in cheese, basil, thyme, lovage or celery leaves, peas, and clams, and loosely cover pan with foil. Continue to cook for about 7 minutes, or until all clams have opened and rice has absorbed all liquid. Serve immediately in pan.

Peas with Fresh Marjoram

4 servings

2 cups shelled peas
2 teaspoons butter
⅛ teaspoon freshly ground white pepper
1 tablespoon minced fresh marjoram

Cook peas until tender. Drain. Return to saucepan. Add butter and pepper and toss until peas are lightly coated with butter. Transfer to a serving bowl and sprinkle with marjoram.

Crackling Chicken with Sugar Snaps

4 servings

    2 whole boneless chicken breasts (about 1½ pounds),
        halved lengthwise
    whole wheat flour for dredging
    1 large egg, beaten with 3 tablespoons water
1¼ cups chopped almonds
    2 tablespoons plus 1 teaspoon corn oil
    2 tablespoons minced shallots
½ cup chicken stock
    1 pound sugar snap peas, trimmed, strings removed,
        and cut into thin diagonal slices
    1 scallion, cut into thin diagonal slices
    1 tablespoon minced fresh parsley
    1 tablespoon minced fresh chives
¼ cup sunflower seeds
    4 whole sugar snap peas for garnish
    minced fresh chives for garnish

Using a meat mallet, flatten each chicken-breast half between 2 sheets of plastic wrap. Dredge chicken in flour, shaking off excess. Dip in egg. Coat lightly with nuts.

Heat 2 tablespoons of the oil in a medium-size nonstick skillet over medium heat. Add 2 pieces of chicken and sauté for 4 to 6 minutes, or until golden, turning once. Transfer with tongs to an ovenproof plate and keep warm in a 200°F oven. Sauté remaining chicken. Wash skillet.

Heat the remaining oil in skillet. Add shallots and cook for 1 minute. Add stock. Bring to a boil over medium-high heat and boil until liquid is reduced by half. Reduce heat to low. Gently stir in peas, scallions, parsley, chives, and sunflower seeds. Heat through for 1 minute. Pour over chicken. Garnish with whole sugar snap peas and minced chives.

Variation: Substitute 1½ cups blanched young peas for the sugar snap peas.

> ### Mature Peas Are Tasty, Too
>
> Older peas are similar to shell beans in taste and especially in texture. These peas can be used instead of beans in burritos, tacos, chili, soups, and stews.

Puree of Peas with Lettuce

makes 2½ cups

Serve with roasted meats or poultry. This recipe is a good way to use older peas.

  1 tablespoon butter
  ¼ cup minced onions
  ⅔ cup chicken stock or water
2½ cups shelled peas
  1 head Boston lettuce, rinsed, cored, and shredded
  2 tablespoons minced fresh parsley
  1 tablespoon minced fresh tarragon
        or ½ teaspoon dried tarragon
  ¼ teaspoon freshly ground white pepper

Melt butter in a medium-size saucepan over low heat. Add onions and cook until soft, about 4 minutes. Add stock or water. Bring to a boil. Add peas and lettuce. Cover and simmer for 3 to 10 minutes, or until peas are tender. Transfer mixture to a food processor, add parsley, tarragon, and pepper, and puree until almost smooth. Serve immediately.

tip

Peas for Dessert?

Of course. What could be sweeter than shelled, tender, baby peas? Toss them with sweet strawberries and honeydew chunks, and dress with thick yogurt that has been flavored with oranges or lime and sweetened with honey.

Arancini with Peas

6 servings as a side dish or appetizer

  1 cup shelled peas
  1 cup arborio rice
  2 cups water
  1 tablespoon minced fresh basil
        or 1½ teaspoons dried basil, divided
  2 egg whites
  1 whole egg
  1 tablespoon water
  2 teaspoons olive oil
  2 tablespoons minced onions
  ¼ cup chopped fresh or drained canned tomatoes
1½ teaspoons minced fresh Italian parsley
  1 tablespoon Parmesan cheese
    about ½ cup fine whole grain bread crumbs
    olive oil
    lemon wedges (optional)
    tomato sauce (optional)

Blanch peas by placing them in a strainer and pouring boiling water over them for 8 seconds. Set aside.

Combine rice and water in a small saucepan and bring to a boil. Cover tightly and simmer over low heat until all water has been absorbed, about 10 minutes.

In a medium-size bowl, stir together rice and 1½ teaspoons of the fresh basil or ½ teaspoon of the dried basil. Beat together egg whites, egg, and water. Stir into rice. Set rice mixture aside.

Heat oil over low heat. Add onions and cook for 2 minutes, or until soft. Add tomatoes, cover, and cook for 10 minutes. Add peas, parsley, and the remaining basil. Cover and cook for 5 minutes. Remove pan from heat and stir in cheese.

Preheat broiler.

Take about one-sixth of the rice mixture and form into a ball about the size of a golf ball. With a spoon, remove some rice from center of ball and fill with about 1 teaspoon of the pea mixture. Re-form ball. Continue making balls (you should have 6). Roll balls in bread crumbs, re-forming, if necessary. Place balls on a baking sheet, and brush with a little oil. Broil them about 4 inches from the heat source, turning often and brushing with oil, until they are lightly browned on all sides.

The rice balls can be served as is or cut in half. Accompany with lemon wedges or tomato sauce, if desired.

Peas with Nasturtium Blossoms and Watercress

4 servings

1 teaspoon olive oil
1 clove garlic, minced
1 tablespoon minced fresh dill
1 cup shelled peas
1 cup watercress, stems removed
1 cup loosely packed nasturtium blossoms

In a large skillet, heat oil. Add garlic, dill, and peas, and sauté for about 2 minutes. Toss in watercress and nasturtiums, and sauté for about 10 seconds more. Serve immediately.

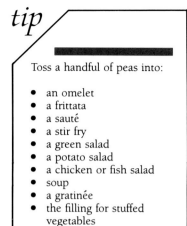

tip

Toss a handful of peas into:

- an omelet
- a frittata
- a sauté
- a stir fry
- a green salad
- a potato salad
- a chicken or fish salad
- soup
- a gratinée
- the filling for stuffed vegetables
- marinated vegetables
- a risotto or cooked rice
- a quiche
- pasta

Pea Custard with Roasted Red Peppers

6 to 8 servings

Serve as a side dish, first course, lunch, or light dinner.

2 roasted sweet red peppers (page 92), cut into strips
1 cup shelled peas
1 cup mild cheddar cheese
3 eggs
½ cup milk
¼ teaspoon dried oregano
¼ teaspoon dried basil
   pinch of dried mustard

Preheat oven to 450°F.
Lightly oil an 8½-inch-round baking dish and arrange peppers and peas on bottom. Sprinkle on cheese and set aside.
In a medium-size bowl, whisk together eggs, milk, oregano, basil, and dried mustard, and pour mixture over peppers and peas. Bake for 15 minutes, then reduce heat to 325°F, and bake for about 20 minutes more, or until custard is set. Serve hot, warm, or at room temperature.

CHAPTER 9

PEPPERS

In the pursuit of culinary happiness, peppers offer endless variety to the world's cuisines. This is, in part, thanks to Spanish and Portuguese explorers who were so fond of peppers they insisted on toting them everywhere. Now they're famous in the cuisines of Mexico, the southwestern United States, Latin America, India, Indonesia, Malaysia, Hungary, France, Italy, and China.

Peppers are also important to Cajun cooks, who know a secret about the flavor of peppers. The theory is that one single pepper offers many tastes. The secret to these tastes is a cooking process called layering, in which an ingredient is added to a recipe at two or three different stages of cooking.

For example, suppose you're making a stew. First add some minced peppers when you're sautéing the onions. Next, add minced peppers during the actual stewing, and finally, add more minced peppers five or ten minutes before the stew is finished. What you will have done is reveal various flavor levels and create a full, well-rounded taste.

INTO THE BASKET

- Pick sweet peppers when they are firm and full-sized and any color. (Most varieties turn from green to red when mature; but some turn yellow; some start and stay yellow; and some turn chocolate-purple.)
- Use a knife or kitchen shears to harvest because pulling could injure the plant. Leave half the stem on the plant and half on the pepper.
- Frequent picking will increase the total yield of peppers per plant.

INDOOR STORAGE

- Peppers will keep for up to two weeks in the crisper drawer of the refrigerator. Below 45°F most varieties will begin to show

High-Vitamin
Red Peppers

Sweet red peppers have more
vitamins A and C than green
ones.

surface pitting and discoloration. Keep the humidity up in the drawer by daily replacement of a damp paper towel.

- For long-term storage, peppers may be frozen or canned. Freezing peppers is simple because you don't have to blanch them first. They may be sliced, diced, minced, or quartered, then frozen on trays. Transfer to plastic bags after the peppers are frozen. Three fresh peppers will yield about a pint of frozen ones. Note that canning procedures and times will vary according to the ingredients with which the peppers are being canned.

- If you've got a crop of particularly tough-skinned peppers, blanch them for about four minutes before freezing. If you don't, the skins could toughen even more.

CULINARY TECHNIQUES

Roasted Peppers

Roasted peppers are sweet, mellow, smoky, and essential to many recipes. Here are four easy methods:

1. Core and seed peppers while whole with a sharp paring knife. Set whole peppers on a broiler pan about five inches below the element. Broil, turning often, until the peppers are well blistered and charred on all sides, about twenty-five minutes. Don't be alarmed if you hear a few "explosions" in the oven. Pop the peppers into a paper bag and close the bag tightly. This allows the skins to steam away from the flesh. Let the peppers steam for about twenty minutes, then strip off the skins using your fingers and a sharp paring knife. If the skins still give you trouble, hold the peppers under cool water, and the skins should slip right off.

2. Instead of the broiler, put the peppers on the grill. Continue with the remaining procedure.

3. Instead of the broiler, spear a pepper with a meat fork and char over an open flame. Continue with the remaining procedure.

4. To roast large amounts of peppers at one time, place them on baking sheets in a 400°F oven and roast for fifteen minutes. Turn the peppers over and roast for another fifteen minutes. Continue with the remaining procedure.

Wrap roasted peppers in foil and refrigerate for several days before removing the skins.

Weights and Measures

1 pound
  = 2 large bell peppers
  = 3 medium-size bell
    peppers
  = 6 frying (banana)
    peppers
3 medium-size bell peppers
  = 4 cups, thinly sliced
  = 3½ cups, diced
  = 1½ cups puree
4 roasted peppers
  = about 1 cup chopped
    or whole

OK, NEXT YEAR

- Varieties that grow well in climates like the northeastern United States are Gypsy, Lady Bell, and Staddon's Select.
- Where climatic conditions are even and consistent, varieties to try are Yolo Wonder, California Wonder, Keystone Resistant Giant, Early Calwonder, and Big Bertha. These varieties are also resistant to tobacco mosaic virus.
- Keystone Resistant Giant and Yolo Wonder perform well where temperatures are very hot.
- According to researchers at Cornell University, varieties that set the most fruit under fluctuating conditions are Gypsy, Ace, New Ace, Canape, and Stokes Early Hybrid.
- Early Prolific Hybrid does well in the northwestern United States.
- Bell Tower, Shamrock, and Tam Bell perform well in arid climates.
- Sweet and hot peppers will cross-pollinate, so separate them in the garden.
- Early-ripening red varieties include Earliest Red Sweet, Staddon's Select, Lady Bell, and Super Set.
- Early-ripening yellow varieties include Yellow Belle and Super Stuff.
- Pimiento is a heart-shaped variety that's good for canning.

Ideas for Roasted Peppers

- Cut into strips and dredge with flour that has been seasoned with oregano and thyme. Dip the coated strips in beaten egg, then sauté in a small amount of olive oil on both sides until golden.
- Cut into strips and toss with watercress, steamed and peeled shrimp, olive oil, lemon juice, and ground toasted cumin seeds. (To toast cumin seeds, heat in a heavy, dry skillet until fragrant and toasted. Then grind in a spice grinder or with a mortar and pestle.)
- Create your own nachos by sprinkling chopped roasted peppers, minced hot peppers, and grated cheese over tortilla chips. Run under the broiler just until the cheese melts.
- Puree with mild chevre (goat cheese), scallions, and curry powder, and spread on split pitas. Broil for a minute or two, then cut the pitas into wedges and serve hot.
- Cut into strips and toss with blanched mushrooms, minced garlic, artichoke hearts, spinach, lemon juice, and olive oil.
- Place roasted halves on a baking sheet and lay a strip of cheese on each half, sprinkle with minced fresh chives, and broil until cheese melts. Serve with crusty bread.

Sautéed Peppers Four Ways

makes about 2 cups

1 medium-size onion, sliced and separated
1 or 2 cloves garlic, minced
3 bay leaves
1 tablespoon olive oil
1 green pepper, cut into very thin strips
1 sweet red pepper, cut into very thin strips
1 yellow pepper, cut into very thin strips

In a medium-size skillet, sauté onions, garlic, and bay leaves in oil for 5 minutes. Add peppers and cook for about 10 minutes more.

Serve any of the following four ways:

1. Stuff peppers inside of 1-egg omelets and melt Monterey Jack cheese over the top.
2. Serve peppers with whole wheat pita points, feta cheese, and olives.

tip

Peppers for Breakfast

- Sauté peppers with scrambled eggs, onions, potatoes, or sausage.
- Slice peppers horizontally to make rings. Then use the rings as a mold for batter breads, spoon breads, or pancakes. Use about 2 tablespoons of batter per ring, then cook as usual. Cornmeal batters are particularly delicious.

3. Serve peppers on an antipasto platter.
4. Add peppers to a glass jar filled with half white wine vinegar and half olive oil. Let marinate overnight. Drain and toss into salads, use on sandwiches, or use as garnishes for cheese platters.

Bell Pepper Burritos

4 servings

1 tablespoon corn oil
1 small onion, minced
1 small clove garlic, minced
1½ cups chopped green peppers
1¾ cups freshly cooked or canned kidney beans,
        drained and mashed (if using canned, rinse
        in a sieve under running water)
1 tablespoon chopped mild chili peppers
½ teaspoon ground cumin
¼ teaspoon dried oregano
8 flour tortillas
½ cup shredded Monterey Jack, cheddar, or colby cheese
    salsa, pepper sauce, or plain yogurt
    chopped tomatoes
    shredded lettuce

In a medium-size skillet, heat oil over low heat. Add onions and garlic and cook until soft, about 5 minutes. Add green peppers and cook until almost tender, 5 to 10 minutes. Add beans, chili peppers, cumin, and oregano. Heat through.

Place a tortilla in a heavy 10-inch skillet over moderate heat and cook, turning frequently, until soft and pliable. Spread 3 or 4 tablespoons of filling down center of tortilla in a band 4 inches long and 1 inch wide. Sprinkle filling with 1 tablespoon of cheese. Turn one end in, fold one long side over filling and roll up. Place in an ovenproof dish. Repeat with remaining tortillas.

Heat burritos in a preheated 250°F oven for 20 minutes, or until thoroughly warm.

Serve accompanied by salsa, pepper sauce, or yogurt, and chopped tomatoes and lettuce.

Pepper Confetti

To create a beautiful, low-cal soup, use a sharp paring knife to cut slender 1-inch slivers of various colors of sweet peppers. Toss them into the bottom of a soup bowl and pour in a clear, hot broth.

You can also cut the peppers into tiny circles or other shapes, using aspic cutters.

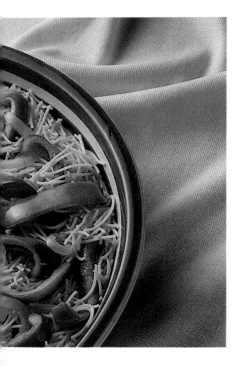

Peppers with Saffron and Pan-Fried Noodles

4 servings

½ pound vermicelli
¼ teaspoon crumbled saffron threads
1 tablespoon hot vegetable stock, chicken stock, or water
1 teaspoon olive oil
1 teaspoon butter
2 cloves garlic, minced
1 bay leaf
1 medium-size sweet red pepper, sliced into thin strips
1 medium-size green pepper, sliced into thin strips
⅓ cup grated Parmesan cheese

Cook vermicelli in boiling water for 7 to 9 minutes, or until al dente. Drain and set aside.

Combine saffron and stock or water in a small bowl and set aside.

In a medium-size nonstick skillet, heat oil and butter. Add garlic, bay leaf, and peppers, and sauté for about 3 minutes. Remove from skillet and add noodles and saffron and sauté, stirring constantly, for about 3 minutes. Add pepper mixture and cheese to noodles and toss to combine. Remove bay leaf. Serve hot.

Pimiento Pizza with Fontina Cheese

8 to 10 servings

4 tablespoons olive oil, divided
1 cup thinly sliced yellow Spanish onions
1 clove garlic, minced
2 medium-size yellow peppers, cut into julienne strips
       ¼ inch thick
2 medium-size sweet red peppers, cut into julienne strips
       ¼ inch thick
½ teaspoon dried marjoram
   freshly ground black pepper to taste
1 tablespoon dry yeast
1 cup warm water (105° to 115°F)

1 cup unbleached white flour
2 to 2½ cups whole wheat flour
8 ounces Italian fontina cheese, cut into ½-inch cubes
  grated Parmesan or Romano cheese (optional)

In a medium-size skillet, heat 2 tablespoons of the oil over medium-low heat. Add onions and garlic and sauté until soft, about 4 minutes. Add pepper strips, cover, and cook for 15 minutes, or until tender, stirring frequently. Add marjoram and pepper. Transfer to a bowl, cover, and let stand at room temperature while preparing dough.

Sprinkle yeast over warm water in a large bowl. Let stand in a warm place for 5 minutes. Stir with a wooden spoon until yeast is dissolved. Stir in white flour and the remaining oil. Add 1 cup whole wheat flour. Dough should be soft and start to come away from sides of bowl. Add more water, 1 tablespoon at a time, if it is dry and crumbly. Turn dough out onto a lightly floured surface. Knead dough, adding more flour, a little at a time. Add only enough flour to keep dough from sticking to your hands. Continue kneading only until dough is smooth and elastic. Form into a ball.

Lightly oil a large bowl. Add dough, turning to coat all sides. Cover bowl with plastic wrap, then a towel, and let rise in a warm place until doubled in bulk, 30 to 45 minutes. Punch dough down. Knead for 1 minute on lightly floured surface. Cover and let stand for 10 minutes. Press dough out to a round shape, then roll out to form a 16-inch circle. Place on an oiled baking sheet.

Scatter fontina cubes over dough. Drain liquid from pepper-onion mixture, reserving 2 tablespoons. Spread pepper-onion mixture over fontina, then drizzle with reserved liquid. Sprinkle with Parmesan or Romano, if desired.

Bake in a preheated 475°F oven for 10 to 15 minutes, or until outer crust is crisp and cheese has melted.

Chili Versatility

Chilies are used in Cajun, Creole, Mexican, African, Thai, Szechuan, Indonesian, and Indian cuisines. They are especially harmonious with eggs, tomatoes, cheese, pork, shellfish, and sweet peppers.

Milder chili varieties include New Mexico 6, Nu-Mex Big Jim, Chimayo, Numex R. Naky, and Tam Mild Jalapeño. Fearless fire-eaters might try Sandia, Cayenne, Colorado, or Habenero, which, according to researchers at Texas A&M University, are 1,000 times hotter than a jalapeño!

Spark a Soufflé; Snap Up a Stew

Cayenne pepper is the dried, ground powder that comes from the Long Red Cayenne Pepper. The walls of the peppers are dried in a slow oven (150°F) until completely dry. They are then ground into powder.

Use a tiny pinch of cayenne in cheese and egg recipes, soups, and Mexican and Southeast Asian food.

Don't freeze recipes that include cayenne because its flavor could become lost and distorted. Instead, add it just before serving.

Linguine with Peppers and Clams

4 servings

    1 pound linguine
   12 littleneck clams
   ¼ cup water
    2 tablespoons plus ½ teaspoon olive oil, divided
    1 clove garlic, minced
    2 cloves garlic, crushed
    1 small hot red pepper
    3 sweet red peppers, thinly sliced
    1 green pepper, thinly sliced
      chicken stock
    8 leaves fresh basil, minced, or 1 teaspoon dried basil
    3 tablespoons grated Parmesan cheese

Cook linguine in boiling water for 8 or 9 minutes, or until al dente. Drain and set aside.

In a large skillet, combine clams, water, ½ teaspoon of the oil, and minced garlic. Cover pan and steam clams over high heat, shaking pan vigorously, until clams open. Remove clams with tongs. Strain liquid through cheesecloth and reserve.

In a medium-size skillet, heat the remaining oil. Add crushed garlic and hot pepper and sauté for 1 minute, or until garlic is golden but not brown. Remove garlic and pepper with a slotted spoon. Add red and green peppers and sauté until peppers are tender but not mushy, about 10 minutes. Measure reserved clam broth (add chicken stock, if necessary) to measure 1 cup liquid. Add broth to skillet and bring to a boil. Add basil.

In a warm serving bowl, toss linguine with cheese. Add sauce and toss. Arrange clams on linguine.

tip

Make a Chili Lily

For your next party, try making chili lilies. Hold a red chili at the stem end and make slits running from the stem end to the point (wear kitchen gloves while you do this). The idea is to make ¼-inch strips in the chili, leaving the stem end and the seed ball intact. Toss the chili into ice water and in several hours the strips will curl back, forming a lily. Use as a garnish for platters, or grouped to make a centerpiece.

Ideas for Pepper Salads

- slices of pepper with ripe tomato chunks, purple onion slices, thyme, lemon juice, and a dash of fruity olive oil
- pepper squares with cooked pasta, chopped green chilies, chopped fresh coriander (cilantro), minced garlic, and a dash of fruity olive oil
- sliced peppers, shredded cooked chicken, ground cumin, ground cardamom, a pinch of saffron, and plain yogurt
- leftover rice with pepper slices, minced ginger root, minced garlic, grated orange peel, rice vinegar, sesame seeds, and a dash of sesame oil
- roasted peppers with shredded mozzarella cheese, chopped fresh basil, and fruity olive oil, served on crisp leaf lettuce
- sliced peppers, cooked baby potatoes, minced chives, minced dill, and plain yogurt, spiked with a bit of dry mustard
- sweet corn kernels, sliced peppers, chopped leeks, minced scallions, minced parsley, crumbled Roquefort cheese, and a splash of apple cider vinegar, served over endive petals
- sliced roasted peppers, chunks of cooked eggplant, crumbled feta cheese, sliced purple onions, minced thyme, minced garlic, and a dash of fruity olive oil, served on red leaf lettuce
- sliced peppers, carrot slices, toasted pine nuts, and minced mint, drizzled with white wine vinegar
- sliced red and green peppers, sliced jicama, and shelled pistachios, sprinkled with orange juice and apple cider vinegar

Bursts of Pepper Stuffed with Shrimp

4 servings

2 large green peppers
½ pound cooked medium-size shrimp, peeled, deveined, and diced
1 teaspoon lime juice
¼ cup chopped celery
2 tablespoons minced green peppers
2 tablespoons minced fresh parsley
1 tablespoon minced scallions
2 teaspoons minced fresh coriander (cilantro)
½ cup plain yogurt, drained for 20 minutes
   lime slices as garnish (optional)

Slice peppers lengthwise on each side of stem. Remove seeds and membranes. Steam-blanch until light green. Plunge into ice water; drain well. Chill peppers.

Toss shrimp, lime juice, celery, green peppers, parsley, scallions, and coriander. Add yogurt and toss again. Chill until serving time, or for at least 1 hour.

To serve, stuff pepper shells with shrimp mixture. Garnish with lime slices, if desired.

Two-Pepper Salsa

makes ½ cup

Serve with omelets or other egg dishes, grilled fish, or corn bread.

1 tablespoon minced fresh coriander (cilantro)
2 sweet peppers, roasted and chopped
1 mild green chili, peeled
½ teaspoon cumin seeds, ground
½ teaspoon dried oregano
½ teaspoon honey
1 tablespoon apple cider vinegar
   dash of ground cinnamon

Combine all ingredients in a food processor or blender and blend until combined and slightly chunky.

Stir Fry of Pork with Three Peppers

4 servings

Serve with rice or skinny Chinese noodles.

1 pound lean pork, cut into paper-thin strips
2 teaspoons cornstarch
1 tablespoon soy sauce
1 tablespoon apple juice
  pinch of ground ginger
2 tablespoons peanut oil, divided
½ sweet red pepper, cut into ¼-inch strips
1 medium-size yellow pepper, cut into ¼-inch strips
1 medium-size green pepper, cut into ¼-inch strips
1 small slice ginger root, minced
1 clove garlic, minced
½ teaspoon sesame oil

In a medium-size bowl, toss pork with cornstarch. Add soy sauce, juice, and ground ginger, and combine well. Let mixture marinate for 10 minutes.

Meanwhile, heat a wok or large skillet over medium-high heat for 1 minute. Add 1 teaspoon of the peanut oil and heat for 1 minute. Add all the peppers and stir-fry for about 1 minute. Remove peppers and set aside.

Add the remaining peanut oil and heat for 1 minute. Then add pork and its marinade, ginger root, and garlic, and stir-fry until pork is cooked through, about 5 minutes. When pork is cooked, add peppers and sesame oil and toss to combine.

Uses for Pepper Cases

Use a hollowed-out pepper as a container for dip, pâté, or cheese spread. When the dip is finished, chop the pepper and toss it into a salad.

Hollowed-out peppers can also hold carrot sticks, celery spears, and olives.

tip

Sweet Pepper Dessert Puree

Use this puree in place of carrot or fruit puree in cakes, quick breads, and muffins or for dessert sauces.

Seed and chop sweet red or yellow peppers and toss into a saucepan with apple juice or white grape juice to cover. Add a cinnamon stick and simmer, uncovered, until the peppers are tender, about 20 minutes. Puree the mixture in a food processor or blender, let cool, and sweeten with honey to taste.

When you're serving applesauce for dessert, mix in 1 part Sweet Pepper Dessert Puree to 2 parts applesauce or use Sweet Pepper Dessert Puree as a base for a refreshing, frozen sorbet.

Ideas for Stuffed Peppers

To prepare peppers, remove tops and seeds. Blanch the peppers for 4 minutes. Drain, stuff, and bake at 375°F for about 20 minutes. Note that you can "blanch" 2 peppers, wrapped in waxed paper, in a microwave for 1½ minutes on full power. For stuffing suggestions, try one of the following:

- chunks of cooked chicken, walnuts, cooked tiny pasta, mild white cheese, and oregano
- sliced sweet onions, cooked barley, chopped mushrooms, Swiss cheese, minced chives, and a dash of freshly grated nutmeg
- chopped cooked shrimp, tomato sauce, whole grain bread crumbs, minced fresh dill, and shredded mozzarella cheese
- day-old, crumbled corn bread, chopped mild green chilies, minced jalapeño, a dash of chili powder, and Monterey Jack cheese
- chunks of crabmeat, minced celery, minced garlic, grated fresh orange peel, and tomato sauce
- cooked lamb, cooked chick-peas, minced mint, chopped tomatoes, minced garlic, and Havarti cheese
- cooked chopped squash, smoked turkey, minced onions, and Swiss cheese

Hot Stuff

makes about 3½ cups

A wonderfully spicy sauce.

 25 hot chilies
  3 onions, sliced
  3 cloves garlic
1½ quarts tomato sauce
  3 cups red wine vinegar
  ½ cup honey

Remove seeds from chilies, using gloves. Place chilies in a large pot with onions, garlic, tomato sauce, and vinegar, and bring to a boil. Continue to boil until vegetables are soft, about 15 minutes. Strain vegetables and discard. Add honey to sauce and continue to boil until thick, about 15 minutes. Let mixture cool and refrigerate.

To can: Pour sauce into sterilized half-pint jars, leaving ¼-inch headspace. Seal and process for 15 minutes in a boiling-water bath.

CHAPTER 10

POTATOES

Potatoes come in two textures, waxy or fluffy, referring to the way their flesh feels when you eat it. Waxy potatoes are generally smaller and are best boiled or steamed and used in potato salads or simply tossed with herbs and a splash of olive oil. New potatoes (the term refers to a stage of growth, not a variety) are an example of waxy potatoes. Fluffy potatoes are usually larger and are best baked or roasted because dry cooking emphasizes their light and airy texture.

INTO THE BASKET

- Harvesting can begin when the vines have died back about halfway.
- A popular way to harvest potatoes is to dig them up with a garden fork. Another way is to dig them up by hand, removing a couple of potatoes from each plant and leaving the rest to continue growing.
- Dig gently—bruised potatoes don't store well.
- Newly dug potatoes are sensitive to heat, so dig early in the day and remove them from the garden immediately.
- If you're planning to store potatoes, cure them first. Do so by placing potatoes in baskets or well-ventilated containers in a shady area between 60° and 80°F. Leave them about four days, or until the skins are dry.

INDOOR STORAGE

- Only store potatoes that are unbruised.
- Keep potatoes in baskets or well-ventilated containers in an area where the temperature is about 45° to 50°F.
- It's best to store potatoes in several medium-sized baskets, rather than one large one.
- If your potatoes are being stored in a garage or cellar with a concrete floor, lay some boards down for the baskets to sit on.

- Keep potatoes free from excessive exposure to artificial light, or they'll develop green patches. If half or more of a potato is green, throw it out. If small areas of green appear, cut them out before cooking. Too much green potato can make you sick.
- Avoid storing potatoes close to apples.
- If the potatoes are going to be stored where last year's crop was stored, give them a fresh start by making sure the area is completely clean.
- When properly stored, potatoes, depending on the variety, will last up to eight months.
- Avoid refrigerating potatoes. Below 40°F a strange taste and dark color could occur when cooked. If you see a dark ring under the skin when you cut open a potato, it means the spud was exposed to freezing temperatures at some time.
- Soft, sprouted potatoes are edible, but pick off the sprouts before cooking.

CULINARY TECHNIQUES

Peeling Particulars

The potato peel contains nutrients but so does the surface just beneath the skin. So, if you must peel, use a swivel-blade peeler and a light touch. Use the pointed tip of the peeler to remove sprouts.

Ideas for Potato Stuffings

- almonds, minced steamed shrimp, and minced fresh chives
- sliced mushrooms, steamed crab, and Monterey Jack cheese
- sharp cheddar, minced jalapeño pepper, minced scallions, and oregano
- crushed pineapple, minced sweet red peppers, minced celery, curry powder, ground ginger, and unsweetened grated coconut
- broccoli florets, diced carrots, corn kernels, plain yogurt, fresh dill, and grated lemon peel
- diced tomatoes, minced onions, minced garlic, fresh basil, fresh thyme, and cooked, crumbled Italian sausage

The Color Controversy

Never cook potatoes in iron cookware—it will turn them an unpleasant blue-gray color.

Nailing Down the Time

Potato nails are four to five inches long and made of metal. Insert them through the center of potatoes (the long way, from end to end), and they'll cut baking time by about fifteen minutes.

The Old-fashioned Way

Mashing potatoes by hand is far superior to electric methods, especially the food processor, which turns potatoes to a gummy mess.

■■■■ OK, NEXT YEAR ■■■■

- Try a seed potato, like Explorer. It offers no chance of carrying tuber-borne diseases like fusarium and verticillium wilt.
- Researchers at Cornell University have discovered that spacing potatoes close together suppresses weeds, as does planting early-growing varieties such as Hudson and Green Mountain.
- What's the best way to get rid of Colorado potato beetles? Entomologists with the Connecticut Agricultural Experiment Station advise picking them off. Drop them in a can of kerosene or squash them. Additional advice includes laying a thick straw mulch to discourage beetles from climbing the plant.
- Sequoia is a variety resistant to leafhoppers and flea beetles.
- A flavorful early variety for boiling is Irish Cobbler.
- Norland is a delicious and early red variety.
- Good keepers include Cherokee, Chieftain, Green Mountain, Plymouth, Katahdin, and Superior.
- Reliable producers are Kennebec, Viking, La Salle, Hudson, and Rural New Yorker.
- Russet Burbank, Early Gem, and Bake-King are varieties that bake well.
- For higher vitamin C and protein, try Butte.
- Flavorful and unusually colored varieties include All Blue, Yukon Gold, Blue Victor, Ladyfinger (yellow), Delta Gold, and Urgenta (pink skin, yellow flesh).
- Rosa, a variety sporting purple spots, is resistant to golden nematodes.
- Don't plant potatoes where they grew last year. Instead, rotate crops—it is best to follow potatoes with legumes.

Weights and Measures

1 pound
   = 3 medium-size potatoes
   = 6 new potatoes (about 2 inches each)
1 medium-large potato, cut into julienne strips
   = 1½ cups
1 medium-large potato, cut into 1-inch cubes
   = 1⅔ cups
1 medium-large potato, cut into ¼-inch slices
   = 1¾ cups
3 medium-large potatoes, shredded
   = 3½ cups
2 medium-large potatoes, mashed
   = 2 cups

Potato Wontons
with Chilies and Cheese

makes 24 appetizers

 1 cup mashed potatoes
1½ tablespoons minced fresh chives
 2 teaspoons mild minced green chilies
 1 jalapeño pepper, seeded and minced
 ½ cup grated sharp cheddar cheese
 24 wonton skins*
  tomato salsa

  In a medium-size bowl, combine potatoes, chives, chilies, jalapeño, and cheese. Place about 2 teaspoons in center of a wonton and bring corners up to form sides around filling. Pinch sides together to form a tulip, and continue with rest of filling and wontons.

  Steam wontons for about 5 minutes and serve with a tomato salsa.

*Wonton skins are available at specialty food stores, oriental markets, and many supermarkets.

Potato and Onion Frittata

6 servings

Great for brunch, lunch, or a light dinner entrée.

  3 medium-size to large potatoes, sliced
  2 medium-size onions, sliced and separated into rings
1½ tablespoons butter
  6 eggs, well beaten
  ¼ teaspoon curry powder
  ¼ teaspoon ground ginger

Steam potatoes for 5 to 10 minutes, or until tender. Set aside.
In a large, heavy, ovenproof skillet, sauté onions in butter until onions are transparent.
In a deep bowl, beat eggs, curry, and ginger. Add potatoes to skillet with onions. Pour egg mixture over all and cook for 5 minutes over low to medium heat. Transfer skillet to broiler and broil 6 inches from heat for about 5 minutes, or until frittata has puffy edges and is a golden color.

Baby Potatoes Filled with Yogurt, Mint, and Dill

makes 8 appetizers

  8 baby potatoes
  1 scallion, chopped
  2 sprigs mint, chopped
  1 cup plain yogurt
  ¼ teaspoon dried dillweed
    paprika for garnish

Steam whole potatoes for 18 to 20 minutes. Drain, let cool, and then scoop about 2 teaspoons of pulp out of each. Set pulp and potatoes aside. Blend scallions and mint with yogurt, dillweed, and potato pulp. Gently put yogurt filing into potato shells and garnish with paprika.

A Note on News

The "new" in new potatoes refers to a stage of growth, not a variety. New potatoes may be harvested anytime, and you can start testing a couple of weeks after flowering. Simply reach into the soil and feel for the size you need, then remove it from the plant.

Potatoes
as Thickeners

Potatoes are a perfect low-fat thickener. Combine 1 part mashed potatoes to 2 parts skim milk, stock, or water, and mix into soups, stews, or sauces. Simmer for about 5 to 7 minutes to thicken.

Roasted Potato Salad with Dill

4 servings

  1 pound new potatoes (10 to 14 little ones), quartered
1½ teaspoons olive oil
  ¼ cup minced scallions
  1 clove garlic, minced
  1 tablespoon minced fresh parsley
  1 tablespoon mayonnaise
  1 tablespoon plain yogurt
  1 tablespoon minced fresh dill

Preheat oven to 375°F.
Pile potatoes into a glass baking dish and toss with oil so that all are coated. Spread potatoes out in a single layer and roast for about 35 minutes. Scoop potatoes into a large bowl and add scallions, garlic, and parsley.
In a small bowl, combine mayonnaise, yogurt, and dill. Add to potatoes and toss well.

Mashed Potato Soup with Potato-Skin Garnish

4 to 6 servings

  2 large baking potatoes
  1 tablespoon olive oil
  1 large onion, chopped
  1 clove garlic, minced
  ⅓ cup minced celery
  3 cups chicken stock
  1 bay leaf
  1 tablespoon grated Parmesan cheese
  ½ teaspoon dried basil
  2 teaspoons melted butter
  1 cup chopped escarole

Bake potatoes in a preheated 400°F oven until they can be easily pierced with a fork, about 50 minutes.
In a large saucepan, heat oil. Add onions, garlic, and celery, and cook over low heat until soft, about 5 minutes. Add stock and bay leaf, and bring to a boil. Reduce heat to low, cover, and simmer

for 20 minutes. Remove bay leaf.

Meanwhile, scoop out insides of potatoes and mash with a potato masher. Cut potato skins into julienne strips. Toss with cheese, basil, and butter. Bake at 400°F until crisp.

Add mashed potatoes and escarole to soup and simmer for 10 minutes.

Garnish with baked potato-skin strips.

Sesame Slices

Cut 2 medium-size potatoes into ¼-inch slices and add them to a microwave-proof dish with 2 teaspoons fresh thyme and 1 teaspoon toasted sesame seeds. Microwave, covered, on full power for 3 minutes. Let stand for 5 minutes, then add a splash of apple cider vinegar, and serve with grilled or poached fish.

Cubed Potatoes with Italian Sausage and Peppers

4 servings

    4 cups cubed (½ inch) unpeeled boiling potatoes
 ½ pound sweet Italian sausage links
    1 small zucchini, cut into ½-inch slices
    2 large onions, thinly sliced
    3 cloves garlic, minced
 ⅛ teaspoon black pepper
    1 small dried hot red pepper, broken in half
    1 large sweet red pepper, thinly sliced
    1 large yellow pepper, thinly sliced
 1½ teaspoons dried basil
 ½ teaspoon dried thyme
    1 can (14 ounces) Italian peeled tomatoes, drained
            and cut in half
       minced fresh Italian parsley for garnish

Steam potatoes for 5 to 10 minutes, or until tender. Set aside.

In a large, heavy skillet, cook sausage over moderate heat until well browned, about 40 minutes. Remove and drain on paper towels.

Add zucchini to skillet and sauté until evenly browned on both sides, 2 or 3 minutes on each side. Remove with a slotted spoon and drain on paper towels.

Add onions, garlic, black pepper, and hot red peppers to skillet. Reduce heat to low and cook, partially covered, until onions are soft and golden brown, about 20 minutes. Stir frequently. Remove red peppers.

Add sweet red and yellow peppers and cook for 3 minutes. Add basil, thyme, tomatoes, potatoes, sausage, and zucchini, and cook for 5 minutes, or until vegetables are tender and mixture is heated through. Spoon into a warmed serving dish and garnish with parsley.

Potatoes Surrounded by Beets and Corn

4 servings

12 baby potatoes, cubed and steamed
 2 small to medium-size beets, scrubbed and cut
        into julienne strips
 1 cup corn kernels
¼ cup white wine vinegar
 2 teaspoons dried mint leaves
½ teaspoon dried marjoram
½ teaspoon anise seeds, crushed
 1 teaspoon safflower oil

Arrange potatoes in center of a serving platter. Surround potatoes with beets and surround beets with corn.

In a small bowl, whisk together vinegar, mint, marjoram, anise seeds, and oil. Drizzle over vegetables.

Eggs Baked in Potato Nests

4 servings

 2 large potatoes, baked
 2 tablespoons plain yogurt
 1 teaspoon dried basil
 1 teaspoon dried thyme
  dash of freshly grated nutmeg
½ teaspoon paprika
1½ teaspoons minced fresh chives, divided
 4 eggs

Preheat oven to 350°F.

Cut potatoes in half crosswise and scoop out most of the potato pulp, making a well large enough to hold an egg.

Mash potato pulp, adding yogurt, basil, thyme, nutmeg, paprika, and ½ teaspoon chives.

Break 1 egg at a time into a small saucer. Slip egg carefully from saucer into potato shell. Spoon or pipe some of the mashed pulp around edge of each potato. Sprinkle a few chives onto egg yolks.

Arrange potatoes in a baking dish. Bake for 15 to 18 minutes, or until eggs are set.

The Potato-Bread Connection

Save the water from boiled potatoes to dissolve yeast and to use in place of the liquids in bread recipes. Potato water may be stored in the refrigerator for up to 7 days, but bring it back to room temperature before using.

Eggs Baked in Potato Nests

tip

Antoinette's Grilled Potatoes

Cut baking potatoes into ¼-inch slices, but *don't cut all the way through*. Leave about ½ inch at the base of each potato. In between the slices tuck a ring of raw onion. Rub the potatoes with fruity olive oil and sprinkle with freshly grated black pepper and nutmeg, making sure some spice gets in between the slices. Wrap the potatoes in foil, place on a hot grill, and cook for about an hour, or until soft.

Ideas for Potato Salads

- chunks of potatoes, capers, basil, and thyme with coarse mustard and sharp vinegar
- slices of potato, garlic, sweet red peppers, and purple onions with apple cider vinegar and peanut oil
- slices of potato with three kinds of greens, freshly grated Parmesan, tarragon, and lemon juice
- chunks of potato, hard-cooked eggs, minced fresh fennel, and a bit of mayonnaise
- chunks of potato, minced garlic, minced ginger root, minced scallions, and sesame seeds with a splash of rice vinegar and toasted sesame oil
- slices of potato, chopped fresh sorrel, baby peas, and a bit of fruity olive oil
- chunks of potato, ground cumin, ground coriander, minced fresh mint, a pinch of dry mustard, and a splash of peanut oil
- chunks of potato tossed with sliced mushrooms, zucchini sticks, and pesto
- slices of potato with minced yellow peppers, walnuts, minced shallots, lemon juice, and a dash of walnut oil
- tiny potatoes, steamed cauliflower, hard-cooked eggs, minced garlic, and grated Parmesan cheese
- tiny potatoes, baby corn, roasted peanuts, chili powder, minced fresh chives, minced garlic, and minced fresh coriander (cilantro)

tip

Cafe St. Michel Potatoes

This concept is adapted from the potatoes served at the restaurant at the lovely Place St. Michel Hotel in Miami.

In a medium-size skillet, warm a bit of olive oil with a bit of butter. Add minced onions, minced sweet red and green peppers, and chopped green olives, and sauté for about 7 minutes. Add paprika, marjoram, and cooked, halved new potatoes and toss to combine. Serve with grilled chicken or fish, or with eggs and grits for breakfast.

Medley of Potatoes, Scallops, and Shrimp

4 servings

1½ pounds unpeeled boiling potatoes, quartered
            and cut into ¾-inch pieces
1 scallion, thinly sliced
¼ cup julienned yellow squash or zucchini
¼ cup julienned carrots
2 cups water
1 slice onion
2 slices lemon
2 sprigs dill with stems
1 sprig parsley
1 bay leaf
¼ teaspoon black peppercorns
½ pound sea scallops
¼ pound medium-size shrimp
2 medium-size tomatoes, peeled, seeded, and coarsely chopped
½ medium-size cucumber, peeled, halved, seeded,
            and coarsely chopped
1 clove garlic
2 teaspoons snipped dill
3 tablespoons lemon juice
3 tablespoons olive oil
2 teaspoons tomato paste
    red or green leaf lettuce

Steam potatoes until tender, about 8 minutes. Drain and cool. In a large bowl, combine potatoes with scallions, squash, and carrots, and chill.

In a medium-size skillet, combine water, onion, lemons, dill, parsley, bay leaf, and peppercorns. Bring to a boil. Reduce heat to low, cover, and simmer for 15 minutes. Strain. Return liquid to pan. Turn heat to low. Add scallops and cook until opaque, about 2 minutes. Remove with a slotted spoon. Add shrimp to skillet and cook until they turn pinkish orange. Remove with a slotted spoon. Slice each scallop into 2 or 3 pieces. Peel and devein shrimp. Add to potato mixture.

Puree tomatoes, cucumbers, garlic, dill, and lemon juice in a food processor or blender. With the motor running, pour in oil in a steady stream, mixing until thick. Blend in tomato paste.

Line a large serving plate with lettuce. Arrange potato-seafood mixture on lettuce. Spoon some dressing over mixture. Accompany with remaining dressing.

Variations:

You can use other poached seafood, such as crab, lobster, or monkfish, to replace scallops and shrimp.

Substitute steamed green beans or julienned celery for carrots and squash.

Potato Cakes

makes 8 cakes

Serve for breakfast with applesauce and yogurt or as an appetizer or side dish with Dijon mustard.

  2 tablespoons olive oil
¼ cup minced scallions
  1 cup mashed potatoes
½ cup rolled oats
½ teaspoon dill seeds, ground

Add small amount of oil to a nonstick skillet and sauté scallions until reddish brown in color. Scoop them into a medium-size bowl and add potatoes, oats, and dill seeds, and combine well. Use your hands, if necessary, to form a stiff dough.

Divide dough into 8 balls. Form each ball into a pancake and fry pancakes in remaining oil, gradually adding teaspoons of oil a little at a time.

Variation: Substitute ½ teaspoon ground caraway seeds for the dill seeds.

Potato Skins

Slice baked potatoes in half lengthwise and scoop out the pulp. (Save for use in sauces, soups, breads, and stuffings. Mashed potatoes freeze well.) Cut the skins lengthwise again, making quarters. Place them skin-side down on a baking sheet that's been sprayed with vegetable spray and bake at 500°F for 7 to 10 minutes, or until crisp.

For flavored potato skins, try adding one of the following combinations:

- grated Parmesan cheese and minced fresh chives
- grated mozzarella cheese, minced fresh basil, and minced tomato (heat again until mozzarella has melted)
- plain yogurt, minced scallions, and minced fresh dill
- ricotta cheese, toasted slivered almonds, and orange zest

CHAPTER 11

TOMATOES

The tomato gardener is easily distinguished from other humans by the blur he creates while gathering his abundant crop. If you've ever been surrounded by more tomatoes than you can shake a stake at, help is at hand.

This chapter is filled with delicious ideas for appetizers, salads, sauces, entrées, condiments, and even desserts.

INTO THE BASKET

If carefree harvesting appeals to you, keep these tips in mind:

- Harvest tomatoes before they become soft, by gently twisting from the stem. Don't pull.
- To insure a high yield, pick continuously.
- For even ripening, use a mulch. Black plastic is excellent for maintaining soil temperature and moisture. It also helps keep tomatoes clean and off the ground.
- If rainfall is insufficient, plants should be watered since even moisture is crucial during ripening.
- Focus the plants' energy into fruit production and early ripening by pruning (removing shoots that grow between two leaf stalks) and staking. (This is true only for indeterminate varieties or for those that keep growing all season. They are the tomatoes generally used for slicing and in salads and sandwiches and include varieties like Better Boy, Beefmaster, Supersteak, and Marglobe.)
- Splitting, cracking, sunscald, and dark leathery patches (blossom end rot) detract from a tomato's beauty, but it's still safe and delicious to eat if you cut out the ugly parts.
- To inspire ripening before the first frost, pinch off blossoms mid to late August.

INDOOR RIPENING AND STORAGE

There's nothing like the flavor and aroma of vine-ripened tomatoes. They also have one-third more vitamin C than tomatoes ripened inside. But if you must harvest early and store, here are some guidelines:

- As long as tomatoes have some red color, they can be harvested and will usually continue to ripen. Tiny, dark green fruits won't ripen at all, but light green, almost-mature fruits will have a better chance.
- Tomatoes ripen at a temperature between 50° and 85°F.
- Do not attempt to ripen tomatoes on the windowsill. They may turn red, but they won't be ripe and flavorful within.
- Ripen green tomatoes by placing them in a fruit ripener or in a closed brown bag with a ripe apple. Check for ripeness in a day or two.
- At the end of the season, ripen green tomatoes by uprooting an entire plant and hanging it upside-down.
- Wrap individual unripe tomatoes in newspaper or perforated plastic and store at about 40°F in a basement or cellar, where they will ripen slowly. Not all will ripen, and you must check frequently to remove rotten fruit. They'll last up to four months and offer a flavor that's far better than store-bought. If you don't want to wrap each tomato, simply spread them on a shelf and cover with newspaper or plastic.
- Ripe tomatoes will keep for two or three days at room temperature.
- Try to keep ripe tomatoes out of the refrigerator because the old will lessen the flavor.
- If you must refrigerate, keep the tomatoes uncut and uncovered, and they'll last about a week. If slightly underripe, they'll last two weeks. Green tomatoes can also be stored in the refrigerator for about two weeks.

DRIED TOMATOES

If you live in a temperate, sunny climate with no humidity, air pollution, or bugs, you can dry your tomatoes outside on screens.

If you live elsewhere, use a commercial dryer. First, blanch the tomatoes for three minutes in boiling water. Then drain and pat them dry. If you're using paste tomatoes, like Roma, halve them vertically. Paste tomatoes have a rich, concentrated flavor, but other tomatoes can be cut into half-inch slices and dried successfully.

Set the temperature for about 150°F and let the tomatoes dry for seven to nine hours, or until they're leathery. Store them in tightly closed glass jars for up to a year.

Reconstitute dried tomatoes by cooking them in a bit of stock until they're soft. Then use them with pasta recipes, omelets, salads, and in sauces and sautés.

CULINARY TECHNIQUES

Four Ways to Peel Tomatoes

To peel a tomato using any one of the following four methods, be sure to use a sharp knife, and remove the skin in strips while holding the tomato gently in your other hand. Don't squeeze the tomato.

1. *The Boiling-Water Method.* Immerse tomatoes in boiling water for thirty to sixty seconds, depending on size. Then plunge into ice water for several seconds.
2. *Strainer Style.* Set tomatoes in a strainer and pour boiling water over them for five seconds.
3. *Microwave Magic.* Microwave one tomato on full power for thirty to sixty seconds, depending on size and ripeness.
4. *The Freezer Plan.* If you've got the room, freeze tomatoes whole. When ready to use, remove from freezer and plunge into boiling water for several seconds. Skins slip right off and tomatoes are ready for use.

■ OK, NEXT YEAR ■

- For early ripening, work in a fertilizer high in phosphorus (and low in nitrogen) in rings around the plants.
- Insure the early survival of tomato plants by selecting varieties that are VFN-resistant (resistant to verticillium and fusarium wilts and nematodes).
- Anxious for vine-ripened tomatoes? Plant an early-ripening variety like Early Girl. The flavor is not as memorable as later-maturing varieties, but they are better than store-bought tomatoes.
- Try a low-acid yellow or orange variety like Sunray, Taxi, or Jubilee.
- Plant a long-keeping variety, like Burpee's Longkeeper. The fruit is orange-red with red flesh and will keep an average of three months in a cool spot. The flavor is superior to store-bought tomatoes.
- For juicing, canning, and ketchup, the Pennsylvania State Extension Service recommends Ramapo, Heinz 1350-1370, Red-Pac, Campbell 1327, and Supersonic.
- Get a health boost from your garden by planting tomato varieties that are naturally high in vitamins: Doublerich and Sweet 100 are high in vitamin C, and Carogold is high in vitamin A.
- Plant complementary-flavored herbs like basil, rosemary, oregano, marjoram, tarragon, and thyme.

How Many Tomatoes in a Pound?

Beefsteak	½ to 1
Better Boy	2 to 3
Big Boy	3 to 4
Early Girl	3 to 4
Pixie	30
Roma	8
Sicilian Heart	1 to 2
Sunray	3
Taxi	3

One pound of tomatoes will yield about 1 cup of pulp after peeling and seeding.

No-Cook Tomato Sauce

makes 3 cups

Toss with thin pasta or serve over fish, chicken, or eggs.

3 cups peeled, seeded, and coarsely chopped tomatoes
⅓ cup minced scallions
1 clove garlic, minced
3 tablespoons minced fresh parsley
½ teaspoon minced fresh tarragon or pinch of dried tarragon
½ teaspoon minced fresh thyme or pinch of dried thyme
½ cup chicken stock

In a food processor or blender, combine all ingredients. Process until well combined but still chunky.

Variation: To make chilled soup, add another ½ cup stock, ¼ cup fresh lemon juice, and 1 cup watercress leaves and process briefly.

tip

Fresh Tomato Cups

Slice off the top of any size ripe tomato, and scoop out the seeds, juice, and pulp. (Reserve pulp for stewed tomatoes or tomato sauces.) Cherry tomatoes can be stuffed with herbed cheese and used as appetizers. Larger tomatoes can be used as bowls for shrimp cocktail, marinated vegetables, pasta salad, egg salad, chilled soup, sorbet, or scrambled eggs.

Grilled Marinated Tomatoes

6 servings

This concept was inspired by Tom Ney, an extraordinary chef and director of the Rodale Food Center.

12 plum tomatoes*
 3 tablespoons rice vinegar
 1 tablespoon olive oil
 3 bay leaves
 2 cloves garlic, minced
 2 teaspoons fresh thyme leaves or minced basil

     Gently seed and drain tomatoes. Grill or broil about 6 inches from heat source, 5 minutes on one side and 2 on the other. The skins will be blistered and slightly charred.

     In a 9-inch glass dish, combine vinegar, oil, bay leaves, garlic, and thyme or basil. Set grilled tomatoes in a single layer in marinade and spoon some marinade over tomatoes. Cover and marinate for at least an hour. The marinated tomatoes will keep, refrigerated, for about 5 days.

     Serve on crisp French bread or crackers, or over rice or pasta.

*Paste tomatoes are best for this recipe but slicing tomatoes, like Big Boy, are excellent also.

West Texas Barbecue Sauce

makes about 2½ cups

This sauce should be painted on ribs or chicken 3 to 5 minutes before cooking is completed. It can also be served as a dipping sauce at the table or tossed with leftover meats and poultry for sandwiches. If doubling the recipe, increase cooking time by 15 minutes.

1½ tablespoons butter
3 scallions, minced
2 cloves garlic, minced
2 stalks celery, minced
2 bay leaves
1½ cups tomato puree
⅔ cup apple cider vinegar
½ cup apple juice
1½ teaspoons honey
¼ cup Worcestershire sauce
15 tellicherry peppercorns, freshly ground
dash of cayenne pepper (optional)

Melt butter in a large saucepan. Add scallions, garlic, celery, and bay leaves, and sauté for about 5 minutes. Add tomato puree, vinegar, juice, honey, and Worcestershire sauce, and bring mixture to a boil. Reduce heat and simmer, uncovered, for 35 minutes. Add pepper and cayenne, if desired, and simmer for 5 minutes more.

Note: If you're freezing the sauce, omit pepper and cayenne and add them just before serving.

Undecided on Which Sauce to Make?

Tom Gettings, the director of photography at Rodale Press, advises peeling and seeding tomatoes and cooking them down a bit until slightly wilted. Freeze this versatile sauce base, and it will be ready when you are.

Tomato Puree, Coulis, and Fondue

- To make *puree,* peel and seed tomatoes and cook them for about 20 minutes. Then puree through a super-fine strainer or in a food processor.
- Tomato *coulis* (cool-EE) is a gently seasoned puree. To make, simply add herbs (basil, rosemary, or oregano, for instance) before cooking the puree.
- Tomato *fondue* is a coulis that has been thickened by long cooking.
- Puree, coulis, and fondue can be frozen and used in sauces, stews, or soups.

Tomato-Basil Torte

serves 8 as an appetizer or 4 as an entrée

Paste tomatoes, like Roma, work best here, but Better Boy are fine if very well drained.

½ cup minced onions
½ cup minced celery
3 cloves garlic
1 teaspoon olive oil
2 cups seeded tomatoes, kept in a strainer until ready to use
⅓ cup minced fresh basil
1 tablespoon minced fresh parsley
⅔ cup grated mozzarella cheese
4 eggs
1 teaspoon Dijon mustard

Preheat oven to 375°F.

In a medium-size saucepan, sauté onions, celery, and garlic in oil for about 5 minutes. Remove from heat and add tomatoes.

In a small bowl, combine basil, parsley, and mozzarella.

Spray a 9-inch quiche pan with vegetable spray and add half the tomato mixture. Next, add half the basil mixture, then remaining tomato mixture followed by remaining basil mixture.

Beat eggs with mustard and pour evenly over torte. Bake for about 40 minutes, or until eggs are set.

Tomato Concasse

A concasse (kon-KAHSS) is a French term for coarse chopping—in this case, coarsely chopping tomatoes. They may be peeled or not, sautéed or not, and they freeze well for later use in omelets, casseroles, soups, or stews. Concasse is a wonderful technique for salad tomatoes and uncooked tomato sauce.

tip

Shortcut
Tomato Paste

Here's a quick way to make plain tomato paste. Peel whole tomatoes and cut and puree them in a food processor or food mill. Then pour the puree into a jelly bag or cotton muslin sack, hang it over a bowl, and let it drip for several hours. Reserve the drippings for soup and freeze the paste remaining in the bag in ice cube trays. Once frozen, transfer the cubes to plastic freezer bags and use as needed.

Tomato Appetizer and Salad Ideas

- coarsely chopped tomatoes with minced mozzarella cheese, fresh oregano, olive oil, and freshly ground pepper
- coarsely chopped tomatoes with chopped zucchini, minced garlic, and fresh oregano
- tomato slices sprinkled with freshly grated Parmesan cheese, olive oil, and minced fresh basil
- tomato chunks, tossed with green chilies, minced fresh coriander (cilantro), and olive oil
- chopped yellow tomatoes with grated white radish, minced ginger root, sesame oil, and sesame seeds
- cherry tomatoes sautéed lightly with garlic and rosemary
- cherry tomatoes, baby corn, minced scallions, chopped fresh flat-leaf parsley, and a dash of curry powder
- chunks of tomato, chunks of chicken, fresh chives, and mustard vinaigrette
- chunks of tomato, chunks of salmon, and steamed baby new potatoes with minced fresh dill and yogurt
- cherry tomatoes, chick-peas, lemon juice, garlic, and thyme
- sliced tomato and green pepper rings with chopped celery and onions, freshly ground black pepper, a dash of cayenne pepper, ground cumin, and olive oil
- chunks of tomato with paper-thin slices of cooked beef, chopped onions, ground coriander, and lime juice
- sliced tomatoes with crumbled feta cheese, chopped walnuts, and fresh chives, sprinkled with walnut oil
- coarsely chopped tomatoes, tossed with cooked rice, minced new onions, fresh chervil, fresh tarragon, and a bit of coarsely ground mustard

Versatile Tomato Puree

When baking, substitute tomato puree for carrot puree or applesauce. The rich tomato flavor adapts surprisingly well to most spices and flavorings.

Flounder with Yellow Tomato Sauce and Fennel

4 servings

Sunray and Taxi are fruity, fragrant yellow tomatoes that work well here. Serve over poached fish or chicken and garnish with fresh minced parsley and minced sweet red peppers.

1 tablespoon fruity olive oil
⅓ cup minced Spanish onions
1 bay leaf
2 cloves garlic, minced

**Flounder with Yellow Tomato
Sauce and Fennel**

2 teaspoons white wine
7 yellow tomatoes, peeled, seeded, and pureed
½ teaspoon fennel seeds, ground
1 pound flounder or other white fish, poached or grilled

    In a medium-size saucepan, warm oil until fragrant. Add onions, bay leaf, and garlic, and sauté for about 5 minutes. Add wine and tomato puree and simmer gently for 15 minutes, stirring occasionally.
    Add fennel and simmer for 15 minutes more, stirring occasionally. Remove bay leaf. Serve sauce over fish.

Uses for Tomato Skins

- Cut skins into even strips and use as ties for small bundles of julienned vegetables like carrots, green beans, celery, squash, or cucumbers.
- Cut skins into flower-petal shapes and use as a garnish.
- Make a tomato rose by cutting a whole tomato skin in a continuous strip. Roll the skin, inside-out, around a toothpick; remove the toothpick and you have a rose.

Pasta with Tomato Cream and Sun-Dried Tomatoes

makes 2 cups

       2 tablespoons butter or olive oil
       2 tablespoons minced shallots
       1 clove garlic, minced
    1½ pounds plum tomatoes, coarsely chopped
       2 long sprigs thyme or 1 teaspoon dried thyme
       1 cup half-and-half or ½ cup half-and-half and ½ cup milk
          freshly ground white pepper to taste
      ⅛ teaspoon freshly ground nutmeg
    1½ teaspoons minced fresh chervil or ¼ teaspoon dried chervil
       6 oil-packed sun-dried tomatoes, drained and thinly slivered
       1 pound vermicelli, cooked

Melt butter or oil in a nonstick skillet. Add shallots and garlic and sauté until soft, about 4 minutes. Add tomatoes and thyme. Simmer, uncovered, until tomatoes are reduced and very thick, about 20 minutes. Press sauce through a fine sieve, discarding herbs. Pour sauce into a medium-size saucepan. If sauce is too thin, simmer until thick, 15 to 20 minutes.

Whisk in half-and-half, pepper, nutmeg, chervil, and sun-dried tomatoes. Heat slowly, stirring frequently (do not let mixture boil). Toss with cooked pasta.

Note: Tomato cream is also delicious served with quiche, scrambled eggs, or poached eggs.

tip

Baked Tomatoes

Slice tomatoes and layer them in a baking dish, sprinkling each layer with basil, oregano, marjoram, or rosemary. Bake at 375°F for about 15 minutes. Serve on fish, chicken, or scrambled eggs.

Herbed Tomato Cheese

makes about 1½ cups

1 cup cream cheese or yogurt cheese*
1 or 2 cloves garlic, minced
1 tablespoon minced fresh chives
1 tablespoon minced fresh dill
1 pound tomatoes (about 4 whole), peeled and gently juiced (you'll
      have about 1 cup)

    In a medium-size bowl, combine cheese, garlic, chives, and dill. Gently fold in tomatoes. Spread on crusty bread or crackers, or fold into an omelet.

*To make 1½ cups of yogurt cheese, let 4 cups of plain yogurt drain in a strainer lined with paper towels overnight.

Pasta with Tomato Cream and Sun-Dried Tomatoes

Cajun Shrimp and Rice

4 servings

This sauce is excellent with eggplant and squash.

Rice:
1½ cups chicken stock
 ¾ cup aromatic rice, like Basmati
 1 bay leaf
 5 mustard seeds, crushed
 1 tablespoon minced fresh parsley

Sauce:
 2 tablespoons chicken stock
 2 tablespoons white wine
 2 cloves garlic, minced
 2 bay leaves
 ½ cup minced red onions
 ½ cup minced green peppers, reserving 2 tablespoons
 ½ cup minced sweet red peppers, reserving 2 tablespoons
 2 cups peeled and chopped plum tomatoes, reserving
     2 tablespoons
 ½ cup minced scallions, reserving 2 tablespoons
 ⅔ cup minced celery, reserving 2 tablespoons
 5 white peppercorns
 5 black peppercorns
 8 green peppercorns
 2 teaspoons dried thyme
 ½ teaspoon gumbo file*
 1 tablespoon chopped fresh parsley
 ½ teaspoon grated orange peel
 1 or 2 dashes of cayenne pepper
15 mustard seeds
 ¼ teaspoon celery seeds
 1 pound cooked shrimp, peeled and deveined

To prepare the rice: Bring stock to a boil. Add rice, bay leaf, mustard seeds, and parsley. Continue to boil for 3 minutes. Cover and simmer for 10 to 12 minutes. Remove from heat, discard bay leaf, and set aside.

To prepare the sauce: Warm stock, wine, garlic, and bay leaves in a medium-size saucepan. Add onions, green and red peppers, tomatoes, scallions, and celery. Simmer for 15 minutes. Grind peppercorns, thyme, file, parsley, orange peel, cayenne, mustard seeds, and celery seeds together. Add to sauce and cook

Uses for Overripe Tomatoes

Although not great for slicing, overripe tomatoes are perfect for sauces, soups, stews, and juices. Tomato dishes made using overripe tomatoes should be enjoyed immediately or frozen but *never canned,* because the pH could be too low to be safe.

for 5 minutes. Add reserved green and red peppers, tomatoes, scallions, and celery. Cook for 5 minutes. Remove bay leaves, gently add shrimp, and serve over rice.

*Gumbo file is dried, ground sassafras root that is used for flavoring and thickening. Do not boil, or it will get stringy. Gumbo file is available at many supermarkets and specialty food stores.

Chunky Salsa

makes about 2½ cups

 2 tablespoons olive oil
½ cup finely chopped onions
½ cup minced celery
 2 tablespoons minced green or sweet red peppers
 2 tablespoons minced hot peppers
 2 cloves garlic, finely minced
 4 medium-size tomatoes, peeled, seeded, and chopped
 2 tablespoons lime juice
 1 teaspoon honey
½ teaspoon dried oregano
¼ teaspoon coriander seeds, crushed
¼ teaspoon cumin seeds, crushed
¼ teaspoon chili powder, or to taste

In a large skillet, heat oil. Add onions, celery, peppers, and garlic. Cook for 5 minutes, stirring occasionally. Stir in tomatoes, lime juice, honey, oregano, coriander, cumin, and chili powder. Bring to a boil. Reduce heat to low, cover, and simmer for 20 minutes. Serve with beans and tortillas, poultry, squash, or fish.

Note: If freezing, omit hot peppers and chili powder and add just before serving.

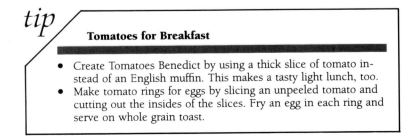

tip

Tomatoes for Breakfast

- Create Tomatoes Benedict by using a thick slice of tomato instead of an English muffin. This makes a tasty light lunch, too.
- Make tomato rings for eggs by slicing an unpeeled tomato and cutting out the insides of the slices. Fry an egg in each ring and serve on whole grain toast.

Tomato Sherbet

8 servings

Delightful and refreshing.

3 cups coarsely chopped tomatoes (5 or 6 medium size)
1 tablespoon lemon juice
½ teaspoon grated lemon peel
⅓ cup honey
¼ teaspoon ground cinnamon
    dash of ground nutmeg

In a food processor or blender, puree tomatoes. Pour through a fine sieve to remove peels and seeds. Measure 3 cups of the juice.

Add all remaining ingredients and mix thoroughly. Pour into an 8-inch-square baking dish and freeze. Stir occasionally to reduce ice crystals. For a smooth texture, process in blender or food processor until smooth but still frozen; pour back into dish and freeze. You can also process again before serving.

Green Tomato Pie

10 servings

Crust:
    ¼ cup unsalted butter, cut into pieces
    ½ cup whole wheat pastry flour
    ½ cup unbleached white flour
    1 to 3 tablespoons apple juice

Filling:
2½ pounds green tomatoes
    1 teaspoon grated lime peel
    1 teaspoon grated ginger root
    ½ teaspoon freshly grated nutmeg
        dash of ground cinnamon
    ¼ cup whole wheat flour
    ⅓ cup dried currants
    ⅓ cup golden raisins
    ⅓ cup shredded coconut
    2 tablespoons honey

Tomato Sherbet

Topping:
  2 tablespoons frozen pie dough (reserved from crust)
  ⅓ cup coarsely chopped pecans
  2 tablespoons maple syrup
  3 tablespoons shredded coconut

To prepare the crust: Combine butter, whole wheat flour, and white flour in a food processor or with a pastry blender in a medium-size bowl until pieces of butter are the size of split peas. Add 1 tablespoon apple juice and continue to combine until dough becomes a solid mass. Add more apple juice, if necessary. Pull about 2 tablespoons of dough from the mass and freeze for the topping. Shape remaining dough into a ball, cover with waxed paper, and refrigerate while preparing the filling.

To prepare the filling: Chop tomatoes into ½-inch pieces. If they are very juicy, drain by letting them rest in a strainer for 1 hour. Combine tomatoes with lime peel, ginger, nutmeg, cinnamon, flour, currants, raisins, coconut, and honey.

Spray a 9-inch pie plate with vegetable spray.

Remove pie dough from refrigerator, roll out on a surface sprinkled lightly with cornstarch, and set into prepared pie plate. Trim edges, if necessary, then crimp decoratively.

To prepare the topping: Grate frozen pie dough into a small bowl. Quickly add pecans, maple syrup, and coconut, and mix to combine.

Fill pie shell with tomato mixture and sprinkle topping over it. Cover pie gently with an aluminum-foil tent.

Bake in a 450°F oven for 10 minutes. Reduce to 350°F and continue baking for 30 to 40 minutes longer.

tip

Five-Minute Microwaved Sauce

In a 1-quart, round, microwave-proof casserole dish, combine 1¼ pounds of chopped tomatoes, 1 teaspoon of dried basil, ½ teaspoon of dried thyme, and 1 clove of minced garlic. Cover and microwave on full power for 5 minutes. Puree in a food processor or blender. Makes 2 cups.

Note: Paste tomatoes, particularly Romas, work well here and give the sauce a beautifully deep red color. Early Girl also produces a flavorful sauce.

CHAPTER *12*

ZUCCHINI

One wonderful thing about zucchini is its hospitality to surrounding flavors. Few other vegetables can so easily take in the tastes and aromas around them. For example, if you toss baby zucchini into a marinade of garlic, thyme, bay, red wine vinegar, and a splash of olive oil, they'll absorb the flavors readily, and there will be no taste clashes, thanks to zucchini's gentle manner.

Larger zucchini can be sliced into spears or coins and used in casseroles, soups, stews, or sautés. Zucchini is harmonious with most cuisines, including Italian, French, Chinese, and Japanese, leaving a wide path for culinary exploration.

INTO THE BASKET

- Zucchini should be picked when it is young—no more than 6 or 7 inches long and about 1½ inches wide. The skin should be tender and dent easily when pressed with a thumb or finger.
- Constant picking will give you a daily supply of delicious zucchini and encourage further production. On the other hand, you can slow down production by allowing one vegetable per bush to continue to grow.
- Avoid plant damage by cutting (rather than ripping) each zucchini at the stem with a sharp knife.
- Keep your eye on the crop—zucchini can grow an inch or more in just one day.

INDOOR STORAGE

- Store zucchini in unsealed plastic bags in the crisper drawer of the refrigerator for up to two weeks. Straight necks generally keep longer than crooknecks.

CULINARY TECHNIQUES

Zucchini Milk

Peel zucchini and cut into chunks. Toss the chunks into a blender or food processor and blend until liquefied. Voilà! Zucchini milk! Use it to replace dairy milk when baking yeast breads, quick breads, cakes, muffins, pancakes, or waffles. It's also great in frozen desserts, puddings, creamy pie fillings, casseroles, soups, and stews. Freeze zucchini milk in recipe-size containers.

Seeds for Snacking

If you decide to let a few zucchini grow to prodigious proportions, use the seeds for snacks. Clean them as you would pumpkin seeds, toss lightly with oil, and sprinkle with herbs or spices, if desired. Then roast them at 375°F for twenty to thirty minutes, or until dry.

■■■ OK, NEXT YEAR ■■■

- Don't overfertilize at planting time or harvest could be delayed by up to two weeks.
- Help discourage vine borers by wrapping an old pair of pantyhose around the stem of the plant where it touches the soil and just beneath the soil surface.
- Early planting can help discourage pickleworms.
- Repel squash bugs by growing radishes, marigolds, or nasturtiums near your zucchini bushes.
- Tinfoil or white plastic mulch will repel mosaic virus–causing aphids.
- Scallopini is a variety that has a pattypan shape with green zucchini skin.
- For a change of pace, try a round variety like Gourmet Globe.
- High-yielding varieties include Burpee Hybrid Zucchini and Onyx.
- French White Bush Zucchini is an early and heavy producer.
- For easy harvesting, grow Aristocrat. The easy-to-see fruit grows straight up.
- If the bees aren't buzzing your plants, you may need to hand-pollinate. Use a small, clean paintbrush to transfer pollen from the male flowers to the female flowers. The male flowers have straight stems, and the females have swollen stems.

Zucchini and Rosemary *Focaccia*

6 to 8 servings

A fragrant Italian bread.

Weights and Measures

3 medium-size zucchini
  = 1 pound
  = 2 cups puree
1 medium-size zucchini
  = 2 cups sliced
  = 1½ cups shredded
2 medium-size zucchini
  = 2 cups diced

  1 tablespoon active dry yeast
  1 cup warm water (105° to 115°F)
  1 tablespoon plus 2 teaspoons olive oil, divided
  ½ teaspoon salt
1½ cups unbleached white flour
1½ to 2 cups whole wheat flour
  ¼ cup minced Spanish onions
  ¾ cup finely chopped zucchini
  1 tablespoon minced fresh rosemary or ½ teaspoon crumbled
       dried rosemary
  2 teaspoons cornmeal
  1 egg, beaten with 1 tablespoon water, for glaze
    rosemary leaves

Stir yeast into warm water in a large, warm bowl. Cover with a towel and let stand for 5 minutes.

Add 1 tablespoon of the oil and stir until yeast has completely dissolved. Stir in salt and white flour. Blend in whole wheat flour, a little at a time, until a soft, sticky dough forms. Turn dough out onto a floured surface and knead until smooth and no longer sticky, adding flour as needed.

Oil a large bowl. Add dough, turning over to coat both sides with oil. Cover bowl with plastic wrap, then a towel. Let rise in a warm place until doubled in bulk, about 1 hour.

Meanwhile, heat remaining oil in a medium-size skillet. Add onions and zucchini and cook until soft, about 5 minutes. Cool to room temperature. Drain off any liquid.

Punch dough down. Knead in rosemary and zucchini mixture.

Lightly coat a baking sheet with oil and sprinkle with cornmeal. Place dough on baking sheet, cover, and let rest for 10 minutes. Press dough into a 10-inch circle. Cover and let rise in a warm place until doubled in bulk, about 30 minutes.

Brush with glaze. Arrange rosemary leaves over top of dough and brush again with glaze. Bake in a preheated 375°F oven for about 45 minutes, or until crust is golden. Cool on a wire rack before serving.

Zucchini and Chicken with Creamy Paprika Dressing

6 servings

1 pound boneless, skinless chicken breasts, poached
3 medium-size zucchini
1 or 2 teaspoons olive oil
1 tablespoon minced onions
¼ teaspoon dried oregano
1 tablespoon minced fresh parsley
1 teaspoon paprika
½ cup sour cream

Shred chicken by hand and set aside.

Cut half of the zucchini into matchstick-size pieces and half into half-moon slices. Combine with chicken and set aside.

In a small skillet, heat 1 teaspoon of the oil. Add onions and sauté for several minutes. Then add oregano, parsley, and paprika, and continue to sauté. You may need more oil if paprika becomes too dry. When mixture is fragrant and paprika has roasted (about 2 minutes), remove pan from heat and combine with sour cream. Toss dressing with chicken and zucchini until well combined.

A Tropical Twist

Freeze blanched and shredded zucchini in pineapple juice—the zucchini will absorb the pineapple flavor. Use in salad, dessert, and bread recipes as you would crushed pineapple.

Warm Zucchini and Sausage Salad

4 servings

1¼ pounds Italian sweet sausage, casing removed
3 tablespoons olive oil, divided
1 teaspoon dried oregano
½ head red leaf lettuce, washed, dried, and torn into
        bite-size pieces
½ small head romaine lettuce, washed, dried, and torn into
        bite-size pieces
2 ounces feta cheese, rinsed, drained, and crumbled
2 cloves garlic, minced
3 medium-size zucchini, cut into ½-inch pieces
2 tablespoons white wine vinegar
12 cherry tomatoes
    freshly ground black pepper to taste

In a nonstick skillet, cook sausage until well browned, turning frequently. Drain on paper towel.

In a small bowl, combine 1 tablespoon of the oil and oregano. Let stand.

Toss greens and feta together in a serving bowl.

Wipe out skillet. Heat remaining oil over medium-low heat. Add garlic and cook for 1 minute. Add zucchini and oregano and oil mixture. Cook until zucchini is tender, about 4 minutes. Add vinegar and bring just to a boil. Immediately pour over greens and feta in bowl and toss well. Add sausage and tomatoes and toss again. Season with pepper and serve immediately.

Squash Blossoms

Zucchini blossoms can be stuffed with fish salads, rice mixtures, cheese and vegetables, or eggs and tomatoes, and prepared according to your favorite recipe. Be sure to pick only the male blossoms (they're the ones with the long narrow stems, as opposed to the females, which have swollen stems). This way the plant will continue to produce.

Ideas for Zucchini Salads

- sliced zucchini, cooked cubed potatoes, cubed apples, yogurt, chopped fresh chives, and freshly grated nutmeg, served in lettuce cups
- sliced zucchini, steamed broccoli florets, minced shallots, chopped fresh tarragon, and balsamic vinegar
- grated zucchini and cooked tiny pasta, tossed with a garlic and basil pesto
- thinly sliced zucchini, tossed with chopped red onions, lemon juice, olive oil, and oregano
- zucchini coins, tossed with tomato wedges, chopped red onions, sliced celery, rice wine vinegar, honey, and soy sauce
- julienned zucchini, surrounded with papaya slices, dressed with lime juice and a bit of honey
- julienned zucchini and halved cherry tomatoes with a dressing of white wine vinegar, Dijon mustard, minced garlic, and minced fresh marjoram
- sliced zucchini, tossed with yogurt, ground cumin, chopped fresh mint, and lime juice
- diced zucchini, cooked cubed chicken, and chopped mango, dressed with yogurt, ginger, cardamom, honey, and lime juice
- sliced zucchini, cooked green beans, julienned green peppers, and pinto beans with apple cider vinegar and a dash of corn oil
- chunks of zucchini, hard-cooked egg, anchovies, minced scallions, and summer savory
- sliced zucchini with peas, sliced mushrooms, minced celery, and minced fresh rosemary
- sliced zucchini with minced fresh fennel, radicchio, lemon juice, and olive oil
- grated zucchini with chick-peas, spinach, olive oil, red wine vinegar, and a pinch of dry mustard
- zucchini spears with a dressing of Dijon mustard, white wine vinegar, snipped dill, and freshly ground pepper
- zucchini rounds with sliced avocado, minced onions, lime juice, and olive oil

A Dieter's Delight

Zucchini contains about 25 calories per cup.

Zucchini "Pasta" with Basil Cream

4 servings

1 cup chicken stock
2 cloves garlic, minced
   pinch of cayenne pepper
1 small carrot, cut into julienne strips
4 large zucchini, cut into 1/8 × 5-inch strips
1/4 cup grated Parmesan cheese
1/4 cup grated mozzarella cheese
1/4 cup half-and-half
1 tablespoon minced fresh basil

In a large skillet, heat stock, garlic, and cayenne to boiling over high heat; cook until slightly reduced. Reduce heat to medium, add carrots, cover, and cook for 3 minutes. Add zucchini, cover, and cook until tender, 1 or 2 minutes. Drain off liquid. Add remaining ingredients and toss until cheeses melt. Serve immediately.

tip

**Zucchini
Chain for Garnish**

Slice zucchini into rounds and remove the centers with a round aspic cutter or a sharp knife. Make a small cut in each loop. Use the cuts to open the loops and link the chain together. Use to garnish platters.

Ecuadorean *Fanesca*

10 servings

A South American spring soup.

2 cups chicken stock
1 cup chopped onions
1 tablespoon fresh oregano
1 teaspoon ground cumin
2 cloves garlic, minced
½ teaspoon black pepper
1 bay leaf
1 cup corn kernels
1 cup peas
1 cup shredded cabbage
1 cup sliced celery
1 cup diced sweet red peppers
1 cup julienned carrots
1 cup green beans
2 cups pureed zucchini
2 cups skim milk
⅓ cup peanut butter
½ cup shredded Muenster cheese

In a large pot, combine stock, onions, oregano, cumin, garlic, pepper, and bay leaf. Bring to a boil and simmer for 5 minutes. Add corn, peas, cabbage, celery, peppers, carrots, and beans, and cook for another 5 minutes.

Meanwhile, in a large bowl, combine zucchini puree, milk, and peanut butter. When thoroughly blended, stir into soup and simmer for another 5 minutes. Turn heat off, remove bay leaf, and sprinkle cheese on top of soup, stirring before serving.

tip

Easy Zucchini Appetizers

- Use slices of large zucchini instead of crackers for cheese, dips, spreads, slices of smoked fish, or poultry.
- Halve a small zucchini lengthwise and remove the seeds with a spoon. Fill with cooked rice, minced scallions, dried currants, yogurt, and curry powder.
- Sauté grated zucchini in olive oil, minced garlic, and minced fresh basil. Combine with grated mozzarella cheese. Stuff the mixture into large mushroom caps and serve.

tip

**Zucchini
Puree to Freeze**

Slice 2 medium-size zucchini and steam for 3 minutes. Drain and puree in a food processor or blender. Spoon into freezer containers and freeze. Thaw before using in soups, stews, casseroles, or breads. Makes 1 cup.

Chilled Zucchini and Avocado Soup

6 servings

4 medium-size zucchini, chopped
2 avocados, peeled, seeded, and chopped
3 medium-size scallions, chopped
½ teaspoon chili powder
½ teaspoon coriander seeds, crushed
2 cloves garlic, minced
1 cup plain yogurt

In a food processor, combine zucchini, avocados, scallions, chili powder, coriander, and garlic, and process until smooth. Blend in yogurt by hand and serve chilled.

Zucchini with Penne Pasta and White Beans

4 servings

1 tablespoon olive oil
1 tablespoon butter
2 cloves garlic, crushed
2 scallions (white part only), thinly sliced
3 medium-size green zucchini, cut into ¼-inch cubes
1½ medium-size yellow zucchini, cut into ¼-inch cubes
2 bay leaves
⅛ teaspoon crushed red pepper
1 cup freshly cooked or canned cannellini beans (rinse and drain, if canned)
⅓ cup minced fresh parsley
½ pound penne pasta, cooked until tender and drained
¼ cup grated Parmesan cheese
¼ cup half-and-half

In a large skillet, heat oil and butter over medium heat. Add garlic and cook for 1 minute. Remove garlic with a slotted spoon. Add scallions and cook until tender, 2 or 3 minutes. Add zucchini, bay leaves, and red pepper. Cover and cook over low heat until zucchini is very soft, about 15 minutes. Remove bay leaves. Add beans and parsley and heat through. Add pasta, cheese, and half-and-half, and toss to combine. Serve immediately.

Fancy Slices

For decoratively striped zucchini slices, score lengthwise with the tines of a fork or a canelle knife before slicing.

Quick Grated Zucchini

Grate unpeeled zucchini and use it in cakes, muffins, and cookies. Or sauté it in stock, olive oil, or butter for about 3 minutes. Let it cool slightly, then pack into freezer containers or bags, seal, label, and freeze. Add, without thawing, to soups, stews, vegetable sautés, frittatas, omelets, crepes, or soufflés.

Zucchini in Pouches

4 servings

2 medium-size zucchini, sliced ¼ inch thick
1 medium-size sweet red pepper, sliced lengthwise, then halved
1 medium-size onion, sliced into thin rings
1 cup corn kernels
½ teaspoon dried basil
¼ teaspoon dill seeds, crushed
¼ teaspoon celery seeds, crushed
¼ cup chicken or vegetable stock

Preheat oven to 350°F.

In a large bowl, combine all ingredients. Divide equally among 4 12-inch squares of aluminum foil or parchment paper, mounding vegetables in the center. Join edges of the squares together at top and seal the open side seams by folding over once or twice. Place on a baking sheet and bake for about 25 minutes, or until zucchini is tender.

Note: Pouches may be cooked on the grill.

CHAPTER 13

APPLES

John Chapman, a.k.a. Johnny Appleseed, was possibly the best public relations guy a fruit ever had. "Apple pies and apple fritters, apple cores to feed the critters," he would sing. To him we owe thanks for filling our autumns with crisp, juicy apples.

The endless search for our roots, both individually and as a nation, has produced renewed interest in the antique apples of Chapman's day. These heirloom varieties have taste and texture appeal and a charming place in our history.

Yellow Newton Pippin, one famous variety, was the first American apple considered good enough to be exported to England. Others include Spitzenburg, Thomas Jefferson's favorite; Sops of Wine, the oldest apple known, dating back to medieval England; Tomkins County King, considered to be the best all-around apple; and Sunrise Rambo, which interestingly is famous for vigorous growth and for fighting disease.

INTO THE BASKET

- Apples are ready to pick when they have good color and aroma. Don't pick immature apples (with green bottoms, for instance), thinking they will store longer. They won't, plus they will taste starchy and bland.
- To pick an apple, hold it firmly in your hand and twist slightly. Take care not to pull the stem out of the apple, or it could rot prematurely. Also avoid ripping the leaves and fruit buds from the tree. Remember, too, that an unbruised apple will keep longer.
- Brownish, spotted areas on apple skins are called russeting and will not affect the taste or quality.

INDOOR STORAGE

Short-term Storage

Refrigerate apples and they will keep ten times longer than at room temperature. Gently place them in plastic bags and spray with water from a plant mister once a week. The apples will last for four to six weeks, depending on the variety.

Long-term Storage

- Apples to be stored for a length of time must be free from decay-inviting bruises.
- Most apples should be kept at 32°F (but not lower than 28°F), because the warmer the storage, the sooner the apples will soften. For example, some varieties will soften twice as fast at 39°F as they will at 32°F. Also note that this cold storage will preserve the apples' nutrients. Some varieties, when stored at 32°F, will keep their vitamin C content for six months.
- Apples that should *not* be kept at 32°F are Mutsu and Northern Spy. Instead, keep them at 39°F.
- Apples should be covered with plastic to inhibit their "breathing," thereby reducing the chances of rotting and softening. Moisten the plastic occasionally.
- Depending on the variety, most good keepers will last in storage for five or six months, and some longer.
- One bad apple *will* spoil the bunch, so check apples frequently.
- Avoid storing apples with potatoes. A rise in temperature could release a substance from the potatoes that will alter the taste of the apples.

▮▮▮ OK, NEXT YEAR ▮▮▮

- Varieties that produce well in low-chill regions are Anna, Dorsett Golden, Michal, Elah's, Maayan, and Shlomite.
- Dwarf varieties to try are Cox Orange Pippin, Maiden Blush, Wagener, York Imperial, and Rhode Island Greening.
- Long-storing varieties include Empire, Mutsu, Newton Pippin, Granny Smith, Jonathan, Caville Blanc, Ben Davis, McIntosh, Baldwin, Lady, Idared, Melrose, Keepsake, Cortland, Nittany, and Goldpairman.
- Caville Blanc is one variety that's exceptionally high in vitamin C. Winesap, Baldwin, Northern Spy, and Summer Pippin are high, too.
- Good cider apples are Golden Russet, Roxbury Russet, McIntosh, Cortland, Ribston Pippin, and Rome.
- Varieties with more than average bearing years are Baldwin, Northern Spy, Ayvanya, Roter Boskoop, Yellow Newton, Black Twig (Paragon), and Splendour.

Apple Salad Suggestions

- chopped apples, watermelon and cantaloupe balls, and grapes, tossed with lemon juice and served in a watermelon basket
- chopped apples, chopped celery, minced scallions, chunks of Jarlsberg cheese, and watercress
- sliced apples, peas, baby onions, sliced mushrooms, savory, and apple cider vinegar
- chunks of apple, pineapple cubes, grapes, ground ginger, walnuts, and yogurt
- sliced apples, raisins, almonds, cooked chicken, and tarragon vinegar
- sliced apples and feta cheese, sprinkled with fresh chives and served on romaine lettuce
- chunks of apple, broccoli florets, grated cheddar cheese, and a splash of sherry vinegar.

CULINARY TECHNIQUES

Perfect Peeling

Vegetable peelers stay sharp for one to three years, depending on the frequency of use. If you replace your peeler when it begins to dull, you'll have no trouble peeling apples. A very sharp paring knife works well, too.

Precise Coring and Slicing

An automatic apple slicer is an inexpensive and handy tool to have around. Slicers are available in both eight- and twelve-section types and can core and slice in one easy step.

Apple-Stuffed Mushrooms

4 to 6 servings

12 medium-size mushrooms (about 1½ to 2 inches in diameter)
½ cup very finely minced peeled apples (use sweet cooking or baking apples)
1 teaspoon lemon juice
2 teaspoons crumbled blue cheese
1 tablespoon finely chopped walnuts, lightly toasted
1 tablespoon fine, lightly toasted whole grain bread crumbs

Wipe mushrooms clean with a soft cloth. Remove stems; reserve for another use. Hollow-out caps with a small spoon.

In a small bowl, stir together apples and lemon juice. Stir in cheese, walnuts, and bread crumbs. Fill mushroom caps. Place under broiler about 4 inches from heat source. Broil for about 5 minutes, or until filling is heated through and lightly browned.

Roquefort-Stuffed Apples

Core whole apples and fill the centers with Roquefort cheese, packed in tightly. Chill for about an hour, then cut into sections and serve. Try it with pears, too.

Apple-Phyllo Kisses

8 servings

1 cup finely chopped cooking apples
1 teaspoon lemon juice
¼ cup grated cheddar cheese
1 tablespoon minced fresh chives
4 phyllo dough sheets
1 to 2 tablespoons melted butter

In a small bowl, combine apples, lemon juice, cheddar cheese, and chives. Set aside.

Preheat oven to 375°F.

Cut each sheet of phyllo in half lengthwise and into fourths crosswise, forming 32 6 × 4-inch squares.

Lay 1 square of phyllo on a sheet of waxed paper. Brush lightly with melted butter. Repeat with 2 more squares of phyllo. Place 2 tablespoons of filling in center. Bring up opposite corners of square and pinch to form a "kiss." Repeat with remaining phyllo. (You should have 8 filled pastries.)

Transfer to a lightly buttered baking sheet. Bake for 15 to 20 minutes, or until golden. Serve warm.

Curried Lamb-Stuffed Apples

4 servings

4 very large baking apples (Granny Smith are nice)
¾ pound lean ground lamb
¾ cup minced celery
¼ cup minced onions
2 cups soft whole grain bread crumbs
½ cup chicken or beef stock
½ teaspoon curry powder
¼ teaspoon ground ginger
¼ teaspoon ground cinnamon
  dash of ground nutmeg

Apple-Phyllo Kisses

Preheat oven to 350°F.

Core apples, scoop out pulp, and finely chop. Reserve ½ cup of pulp.

In a medium-size skillet, brown lamb. Remove with a slotted spoon. Add celery and onions and sauté for 5 minutes, or until tender. Stir in reserved apple pulp and cook for 2 or 3 minutes more. Return lamb to the skillet along with bread crumbs, stock, curry powder, ginger, cinnamon, and nutmeg. Mix well and stuff apples with the mixture.

Place apples in an 8-inch baking dish that has been sprayed with vegetable spray and bake for 35 to 40 minutes, or until apples are tender.

Keep Apples from Browning

Keep cut apples from browning by tossing them in lemon juice.

Ideas for Using Apple Cider and Juice

- Mix half cider or juice and half stock together to make a poaching liquid for fish and chicken.
- Use cider or juice instead of ice water in a pie crust.
- Use cider or juice to make apple jelly.
- Combine cider or juice with strawberry preserves, cook down, and use as a glaze for fruit tarts and pastries.
- Add cider or juice to marinades for added sweetness.
- Use apple juice to replace the liquid in hot cereals and batter breads.

Swiss Chard Filled with Apples and Rice

4 servings

12 to 15 large Swiss chard leaves
1 teaspoon corn oil
1 medium-size onion, finely chopped
1 cup cooked brown rice
½ cup grated Swiss cheese
½ teaspoon freshly grated nutmeg
⅛ teaspoon freshly ground white pepper, or to taste
2 cups finely chopped, peeled cooking apples, tossed
          with 2 teaspoons lemon juice
¼ cup apple juice
¼ cup chicken stock
2 bay leaves
3 black peppercorns

With a paring knife, shave off excess rib from center of each chard leaf down to stem. Cut off stems. Steam chard leaves until bright green and flexible enough to roll. Drain, then dry on paper towels.

Heat oil in a nonstick skillet. Add onions and cook until soft, about 5 minutes. Remove from heat and stir in rice, cheese, nutmeg, pepper, and apples.

Place 2 tablespoons of filling on center of each leaf. Fold up stem ends, then fold sides over filling, then roll up leaf to form a packet. Place filled leaves in an 8-inch baking dish.

Swiss Chard Filled with Apples and Rice

Combine juice, stock, bay leaves, and peppercorns. Pour over chard leaves. Cover tightly with aluminum foil. Bake at 350°F for 20 to 25 minutes, or until leaves are tender and filling is heated through. Baste 2 or 3 times while baking. Remove bay leaves and serve with pan juices spooned over each serving.

tip

Storing Cider

Cider will keep, refrigerated, for about a week. For longer storage, you'll find cider freezes very nicely, and when defrosted, it tastes very much like fresh cider. To freeze, simply pour the cider into freezer containers, leave 2 inches of headspace, seal, and freeze. The cider will last for up to a year.

To can cider, pour into sterilized canning jars, leaving ¼-inch headspace. Seal and place into a canner filled with enough water to cover the jars. Heat the water to 170°F and hold that temperature for 10 minutes. Remove the jars from the water, cool, check seals, and store.

tip

The Three-Minute Apple

Create a quick, nutritious, low-calorie dessert by baking an apple in the microwave. Peel the top third to prevent the insides from bursting through the skin as the heat expands them. Cover the apple and cook on full power for 3 minutes. Serve with plain yogurt, flavored with maple syrup and vanilla.

Apple-Glazed Pork Chops

4 servings

¾ cup apple juice
3 tablespoons lemon juice
1 small onion, minced
1½ tablespoons minced fresh savory or 1½ teaspoons dried savory
4 center-cut pork chops
¼ cup applesauce
1 unpeeled red cooking apple, sliced ½ inch thick
1 unpeeled tart green apple, sliced ½ inch thick

In a shallow dish, combine apple juice, lemon juice, onions, and savory. Add pork chops, turning to coat both sides. Cover and chill for at least 6 hours or overnight. Turn occasionally.

Remove pork chops from marinade. Strain marinade and reserve. Place pork chops on rack of broiler pan. Bake in a preheated 375°F oven for 20 minutes.

Meanwhile, combine 3 tablespoons of marinade with applesauce. Brush pork chops with mixture. Increase oven temperature to 400°F and bake pork chops for 20 to 30 minutes longer, or until done, brushing frequently with applesauce mixture.

In a medium-size skillet, cook sliced apples in remaining marinade until tender.

To serve, arrange pork chops on a heated plate and place sliced apples over chops. Spoon heated marinade over or serve on the side.

Sautéed Chicken and Apples

4 servings

1 tablespoon olive oil
1 tablespoon butter
½ pound boneless, skinless chicken breasts, pounded to flatten slightly
1 medium-size shallot, minced
1 clove garlic, minced
1 tablespoon minced fresh parsley
½ cup sliced celery (1 × ¼-inch pieces)
¼ cup apple juice

¼ cup chicken stock
¼ cup julienned carrots
¼ cup julienned butternut squash
2 large tart cooking apples, peeled, sliced ¼ inch thick,
     and tossed with 2 teaspoons lemon juice
½ teaspoon crumbled dried rosemary
⅛ teaspoon ground mace
   minced fresh chives for garnish (optional)

Heat oil and butter in a large skillet over medium-high heat. Add chicken and lightly brown on both sides. Add shallots, garlic, parsley, and celery, and cook for about 10 seconds, stirring constantly. Add apple juice and stock and cook until liquid is reduced by half. Lower heat to medium-low and add carrots, squash, apples, rosemary, and mace. Cover and cook, stirring frequently and turning chicken over, for about 5 minutes, or until chicken tests done and vegetables are tender.

Remove chicken and cut diagonally into thick slices. Spoon some sauce and vegetables on individual serving plates. Arrange chicken on top. Spoon more sauce and apples on top of chicken. Garnish with chives, if desired.

Apple-Couscous Pudding

4 servings

This recipe also makes a great breakfast.

1 cup milk
1 cup apple juice
1 tablespoon honey
1 tablespoon butter
2 inches stick cinnamon
¼ teaspoon freshly grated nutmeg
1 cup couscous
1 cup chopped, peeled tart apples (such as Granny Smith)
¼ cup chopped, pitted dates

Preheat oven to 350°F.
In a medium-size saucepan, combine milk, juice, honey, butter, cinnamon stick, and nutmeg. Heat just to boiling. Stir in couscous, apples, and dates. Heat until bubbles appear at edges of pan. Remove cinnamon stick and turn into a buttered 1½-quart casserole dish. Bake for 25 to 30 minutes, or until top is lightly browned. Serve warm.

Freezing Apple Slices

To freeze apples, peel, core, slice, and blanch for 2 minutes in boiling water. Cool the slices quickly in ice water, drain, pat dry, and store in freezer bags.

Use the slices, straight from the freezer, in fruit stews, pies, tarts, and compotes or spiced to accompany roasted meats and poultry.

The color and texture of frozen slices in most apple varieties are good. Empire and Stayman frozen slices maintain the best taste; Granny Smith becomes slightly metallic.

Apple Snow

makes about 3 cups

3 medium-size apples, peeled, cored, and chopped
2 cups white grape juice, pear juice, or apple juice
2 tablespoons lime juice

In a food processor or blender, blend all ingredients until you have a smooth puree. (If you're using a blender, you may need to do this in batches.)

Pour puree into a freezer container and freeze overnight. Process again before serving.

Variations:

Add 1 teaspoon of ground cinnamon during processing.

Substitute orange juice for the grape, pear, or apple juice.

Substitute 1 cup of strawberries (fresh or frozen) for 1 of the apples.

Apple-Ginger Strudel

makes 2 pastries, serving 8

Pastry:
½ cup whole wheat pastry flour
½ cup unbleached white flour
½ cup butter, softened
½ cup plain yogurt

Filling:
4 cups thinly sliced, peeled sweet baking apples
1 tablespoon lemon juice
½ cup golden raisins
⅓ cup ground almonds
3 tablespoons honey
3 tablespoons maple syrup
1 teaspoon finely grated lemon peel
1 teaspoon ground ginger

To prepare the pastry: In a small bowl, stir together whole wheat flour and white flour. Cut in butter with pastry blender. Add yogurt and, using your hands, mix well. Form dough into a ball, flatten slightly, and dust with flour. Wrap with waxed paper and chill for 8 hours, or overnight.

To prepare the filling: In a large bowl, toss apples with lemon juice. Add raisins, almonds, honey, maple syrup, lemon peel, and ginger.

Divide dough in half. On a lightly floured surface with a floured rolling pin, roll out one-half of the dough to a 14 × 8-inch rectangle. Spread half of the filling over dough. Starting from the short side, carefully roll up dough, jelly-roll fashion. Using a metal spatula, transfer dough to a baking sheet that has been lightly coated with vegetable spray, seam-side down. With a sharp knife, cut ½-inch slashes into dough at 1-inch intervals. Repeat with remaining dough.

Bake in a preheated 350°F oven for about 25 to 30 minutes, or until lightly browned. Place pastries on a wire rack to cool slightly. Serve warm.

Chunky Baked Apples

6 to 8 servings

 6 medium-size apples, peeled, cored, and chopped
¼ cup whole wheat flour
¼ cup finely chopped walnuts
⅓ cup maple syrup
½ teaspoon grated orange peel
½ teaspoon ground cinnamon
¼ cup half-and-half
　 dash of ground ginger
3 tablespoons grated sharp cheddar cheese

Preheat oven to 450°F. Spray an 8-inch baking dish with vegetable spray.

Combine apples, flour, walnuts, syrup, orange peel, cinnamon, half-and-half, and ginger in prepared dish. Bake for 10 minutes. Reduce heat to 350°F and bake for 20 minutes more. Sprinkle cheese on top and continue to bake for about 10 minutes, or until cheese has melted.

Note: You can make a delicious topping for this dish by combining 1 teaspoon maple syrup with ⅓ cup plain yogurt and a dash of ground cinnamon.

Apples for Breakfast

Toss grated or chunked apples into pancake batter, crepe batter, omelets, scrambled eggs, hot cereals, and cold cereals. Or sauté slices with spicy, lean country sausage.

CHAPTER *14*

GRAPES

Grapes have been pleasing palates and poets for thousands of years. They're friendly fruits that can easily save an otherwise monotonous dish.

Grapes and fish are a famous couple, called *Veronique* in France. But grapes are also outstanding in stuffings for poultry, tossed with pasta and mild white cheese, or sautéed with veal, chicken, or duck.

Cheers to grapes for continuing to tickle our taste buds.

INTO THE BASKET

- Grapes should be picked when they are plump, full size, and aromatic. Observe the color, too. Green grapes should be golden green; red grapes, red; black grapes, a rich blue-black.
- Test for ripeness by gently tugging a grape from the vine. If it comes away easily, it's ready, and you can snip the whole bunch from the vine with shears.
- Grape leaves can be snipped from the vine anytime after they're big enough to fill and roll.

INDOOR STORAGE

- Freshly picked grapes will keep, uncovered, in the refrigerator for about a week.
- During storage, keep your grapes away from other fruits and vegetables because they absorb surrounding odors easily.
- Grape leaves will keep for about a month, wrapped in aluminum foil and sealed in a plastic bag.

CULINARY TECHNIQUES

Simple Slicing and Seeding

Grapes should be sliced with a very sharp knife, or they'll squash. They can also be snipped into halves with kitchen shears; then use the point of the shears to remove the seeds.

155

Weights and Measures

1 pound medium-size
grapes, stemmed
    = 2½ cups
    = 2½ cups halved
    = 2 cups chopped
    = 1½ cups puree

▰▰▰ OK, NEXT YEAR ▰▰▰

- Concord is a good, all-around variety. It tastes good both raw and cooked, juices well, freezes well, keeps well, and grows well in most climates.
- Cold-hardy varieties include St. Croix, Kay Gray, Van Buren, Worden, Edelweiss, and Swenson Red.
- Muscadine vines are good for hot, humid climates. Varieties for general use include Noble, Scuppernong, Southland, Sterling, and Summit.
- Seedless varieties include Thompson, Canadice, Interlaken, Himrod, Suffolk Red, Glenora, Lakemont, Remaily, Vanessa, and Romulus.
- Thompson seedless is a good grape from which to make raisins.
- Help control mildew with attentive pruning—air should be able to circulate around the leaves.

Grapes with Orange Sections and Orange Cream

4 servings

1 cup plain yogurt
1 pound seedless grapes
2 oranges, peeled, pitted, and sectioned
¼ cup finely minced red onions
½ teaspoon grated orange peel
1 teaspoon orange juice concentrate
1 tablespoon finely grated coconut

Scoop yogurt into a strainer that has been lined with a coffee filter or paper towel, and let it drain for about an hour.

Meanwhile, in a serving bowl, combine grapes, orange sections, and onions.

When yogurt is ready (you'll have about ½ cup), gently fold in orange peel, orange concentrate, and coconut, and add to the serving bowl. Combine well and serve.

Baked Brie
with Almonds and Grapes

8 to 10 servings

  1 8-inch round Brie cheese (about 1 pound)
¼ cup sliced almonds, lightly toasted
½ cup chopped green and red seedless grapes
  2 tablespoons white grape juice, divided
  3 tablespoons chopped almonds, lightly toasted

Preheat oven to 400°F.

Cut Brie in half crosswise. Place bottom half in a 10-inch quiche dish or pie plate. Top with sliced almonds, pressing them slightly into cheese. Arrange grapes on top of nuts. Place other half of Brie on top of grapes. Brush top and sides of cheese with 1 tablespoon of the juice. Sprinkle chopped almonds on top. Gently pour the remaining grape juice over top and bake for 3 or 4 minutes, or until cheese is heated through but still retains its shape. With a spatula, transfer to an attractive serving dish. Serve immediately with crackers, crusty bread, or crisp apple slices.

Calorie Count

One cup of grapes is about 100 calories.

Ideas for Grape Salads

- honeydew melon balls, halved black grapes, lime juice and peel, and mint leaves
- blueberries and green grapes with cinnamon-yogurt dressing
- halved green grapes, diced mango, and orange juice with honey-cardamom dressing
- orange-grape salad with pureed raspberry-honey dressing
- cantaloupe balls and red grapes with a yogurt, ginger, and honey dressing
- new potatoes, grapes, and crumbled Roquefort cheese with mustard-honey vinaigrette
- green grapes and sliced Italian plums with French dressing
- grapes, diced pears, and diced celery, served in a cored head of Boston lettuce with orange yogurt
- diced pineapple, sliced kiwi fruit, and red grapes with a pureed strawberry, lemon juice, and honey dressing
- cracked wheat, minced celery, minced scallions, toasted walnuts, a dash of cinnamon, and grapes with a clear vinaigrette
- cooked millet, grapes, water chestnuts, rice vinegar, and sesame oil
- oranges, grapes, and bananas with yogurt, nutmeg, and honey

Breast of Duck with Grape Sauce

4 servings

  1 teaspoon sweet butter
  2 shallots, finely minced
  4 duck breasts*
⅔ cup white grape juice
    pinch of dried thyme
¼ teaspoon Dijon mustard

     Melt butter in a large skillet. Add shallots and sauté for about a minute. Add duck and sauté until both sides have browned and juices run clear when pressed with a spatula, about 4 or 5 minutes. Remove duck to a heated platter and add grape juice and thyme to the skillet. Bring juice to a boil and continue to boil while scraping up the browned bits at bottom with a spatula. When amount of liquid has been reduced by half and has browned and thickened, whisk in mustard, pour over duck, and serve.
     If desired, serve with bunches of chilled fresh grapes.

*If duck breasts are more than ½ inch thick, slice each lengthwise into 2 thinner pieces. If duck is too thick, it could become tough before it cooks.

Variation: Substitute boned chicken breast for the duck, making sure chicken is no more than ½ inch thick.

tip

Grape Chiller

Combine 2 cups purple grape juice and 2 cups orange juice and chill. Serve in tall, frosty glasses garnished with mint.

Soba with Grapes and Ginger-Peanut Dressing

4 servings

½ pound soba noodles
3 teaspoons sesame oil, divided
1½ cups seedless grapes, halved
6 scallions, cut into julienne strips
2 small slices ginger root, finely minced
2 cloves garlic, finely minced
2 tablespoons peanut butter
3 tablespoons white grape juice

Cook soba noodles according to package directions, drain, and toss thoroughly with 1 teaspoon oil. Pour into a serving bowl, add grapes and scallions (reserve 1 tablespoon for garnish), and toss to combine.

In a small bowl, combine ginger, garlic, peanut butter, the remaining oil, and grape juice. Pour over soba noodles and toss until well combined. Sprinkle with reserved scallions and serve.

Variation: Substitute thin pasta for soba noodles.

Shrimp Veronique

4 servings

1 pound large shrimp, shelled
2 tablespoons white grape juice
2 tablespoons raspberry vinegar
2 teaspoons sweet butter
2 tablespoons finely minced onions
2 tablespoons finely minced carrots
2 tablespoons finely minced celery
¼ cup minced fresh parsley
1 tablespoon minced fresh thyme
⅔ cup small seedless grapes
2 tablespoons grated Parmesan cheese

Slice shrimp in half lengthwise by placing each one flat on a cutting board. Place one hand flat on top of shrimp to hold it steady and, using a sharp knife, slice it through. Repeat this process until all shrimp have been halved. Then scoop them into a glass bowl and pour in grape juice and vinegar. Let shrimp marinate for 30 minutes.

Melt butter in a large skillet. Add onions, carrots, celery, parsley, and thyme, and sauté for about 2 minutes. Add shrimp and its marinade and the grapes, and continue to sauté until shrimp are opaque, about 3 minutes. Mix in cheese and serve.

Chicken with Grapes and Curried Mayonnaise

4 servings

Salad:
3½ cups red and green seedless grapes
2½ cups slivered cooked chicken (2 × ¼-inch pieces)
½ cup diced sweet red peppers
1 small papaya, peeled, thinly sliced, and tossed with
       1 teaspoon lemon juice

Dressing:
½ teaspoon curry powder
½ teaspoon honey
2 teaspoons water
1½ teaspoons apple cider vinegar
⅓ cup mayonnaise
⅓ cup plain yogurt

   soft green- and red-tipped lettuce leaves for garnish

To prepare the salad: In a large bowl, combine grapes, chicken, peppers, and papaya. Cover and chill.

To prepare the dressing: In a small skillet, heat curry powder over low heat for 2 or 3 minutes, stirring constantly. Remove from heat and cool.

In a small bowl, whisk together curry, honey, water, and vinegar until honey dissolves. Whisk in mayonnaise and yogurt until well blended. Add two-thirds of dressing to grape-chicken mixture and toss gently.

Arrange lettuce leaves on a chilled salad platter. Mound chicken mixture in center. Serve with remaining dressing on the side.

Ideas for Stuffing Grape Leaves

1. If leaves are fresh, wash well in warm water and trim off stem end. Soften leaves by steaming or boiling for 3 minutes. Drain well and set them, shiny-side down, with stem end facing you. If you're using preserved grape leaves, place in a large bowl and pour hot water over them. Drain, rinse, and let cool.

2. Prepare the stuffing. Suggestions for stuffings include:

   - cooked lentils, cooked rice, chopped dried apricots, minced fresh savory, and minced fresh mint
   - cooked barley, cooked minced chicken, minced scallions, minced celery, and minced carrots
   - cooked rice, minced onions, toasted pine nuts, raisins, dried currants, freshly ground allspice, and minced fresh dill
   - ground lamb or beef, cooked and drained; minced onions; chopped fresh mint; chopped fresh dill; and lemon juice

3. Place a rounded tablespoonful of stuffing in the center of the leaf and fold the stem end over it. Next, fold in the sides of the leaf. Then, roll it up into a little cigar.

4. To cook the stuffed leaves, line the bottom of a large, heavy saucepan with several unused leaves. Then set the stuffed leaves in, seam-side down. Top with several lemon slices and repeat the layering. Invert a heavy, heatproof plate on top of the rolls to keep them from sliding while cooking. Then pour in enough boiling water or stock to come within 1-inch of the saucepan rim. Cover, then simmer for about 40 minutes, or until most of the liquid has been absorbed. The leaves will be tender but chewy.

Dessert Sauce

makes about 1⅓ cups

Serve this sauce with cake, ice cream, or fruit.

2 cups black seedless grapes
1 tablespoon lemon juice
½ teaspoon lemon peel
1 small slice ginger root
2 inches stick cinnamon
3 or 4 tablespoons honey, according to taste
½ cup water
1 teaspoon cornstarch, mixed with 2 teaspoons cold water

In a small saucepan, combine grapes, lemon juice and peel, ginger, cinnamon, honey, and water. Bring to a boil. Stir in cornstarch mixture. Cook until thickened, stirring constantly. Remove cinnamon stick. Serve warm or chilled.

Grape Leaves for Crisper Pickles

Two grape leaves added to a quart of salt-free cucumber pickles before canning will help preserve crispness.

Easy Grape Ice

4 servings

¼ cup purple grape juice
¼ cup white grape juice
½ cup apple juice concentrate
1 tablespoon honey
2 teaspoons lime juice
1½ cups ice cubes

In a food processor or blender, combine grape juices, apple juice concentrate, honey, and lime juice. Chill thoroughly and then blend until thoroughly mixed. Add ice cubes and blend at high speed until mixture has a snowy consistency. Serve at once.

Note: Create another frozen treat by freezing whole, stemmed grapes. Eat them straight from the freezer. They're like candy without the calories.

CHAPTER *15*

PEACHES

Are you accustomed to repeating those old standards, peach pie, peach cobbler, and peaches and cream, over and over every year? If so, you'll be pleased to discover what peaches have been up to lately.

In the new, garden-fresh kitchen, the clingstone types of peaches, which have a firm flesh (and according to some gardeners, better flavor than freestone varieties), are sliced off the stone and sautéed with slivers of marinated pork or plump shrimp, adding color, flavor, and texture. You can also chop them finely to add to risotto, rice pilaf, or poultry stuffing.

The juicier flesh of freestone peaches is wonderful pureed in a blender and used as a natural sweetener in marinades, sauces, and glazes for roast meats and poultry. Try it in a teriyaki-type marinade in place of your normal sweetener, and you'll be entranced by its flavor and perfume. Do note that when using peach puree in an uncooked sauce, always add an acid to maintain the puree's color. For each cup of puree, add one-half to one teaspoon of lime juice, lemon juice, orange juice, or mild-tasting vinegar. Peach puree will also enliven cakes and quick breads. Simply substitute one-third of the recipe's liquid with peach puree and cut down on the sweetener to taste. Then bake as usual.

INTO THE BASKET

- Peaches are ready to pick when the last remainder of green has turned to yellow. When peaches are first ripe, the flesh at the end away from the stem gives *slightly* to thumb pressure. This is called firm-ripe. When the flesh at the end away from the stem yields *well* to thumb pressure, peaches are tree-ripe.
- Avoid brown rot by picking promptly. If peaches are left on the tree long after the tree-ripe stage, their skins become soft and invite brown rot.
- To pick a peach without bruising it or damaging the tree, cup it in your hand, lift, and slightly twist. The stem should come away clean, rather than tearing as it would if you pulled it straight off.

Weights and Measures

1 pound peaches
= 2 or 3 whole
= 1½ cups sliced
= 1⅔ cups chopped
= 1½ cups puree

INDOOR RIPENING AND STORAGE

- Peaches at the firm-ripe stage will keep, refrigerated, for about two weeks. Spread them out in one layer to minimize bruising. Then bring them out and they'll ripen to excellent flavor and texture in one or two days out of sunlight at room temperature.
- Tree-ripe peaches will keep, refrigerated, for a few days.

CULINARY TECHNIQUES

Two Ways to Peel Peaches

1. Dunk peaches into boiling water for about thirty seconds. Then quickly transfer the peaches to ice water. Remove from water and slip skins off. If the peaches are not quite ripe, you may need a sharp paring knife to get the peeling started.

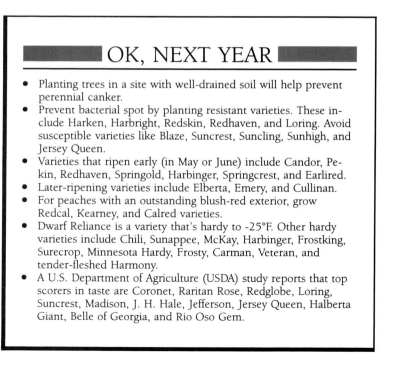

██ OK, NEXT YEAR ██

- Planting trees in a site with well-drained soil will help prevent perennial canker.
- Prevent bacterial spot by planting resistant varieties. These include Harken, Harbright, Redskin, Redhaven, and Loring. Avoid susceptible varieties like Blaze, Suncrest, Suncling, Sunhigh, and Jersey Queen.
- Varieties that ripen early (in May or June) include Candor, Pekin, Redhaven, Springold, Harbinger, Springcrest, and Earlired.
- Later-ripening varieties include Elberta, Emery, and Cullinan.
- For peaches with an outstanding blush-red exterior, grow Redcal, Kearney, and Calred varieties.
- Dwarf Reliance is a variety that's hardy to -25°F. Other hardy varieties include Chili, Sunappee, McKay, Harbinger, Frostking, Surecrop, Minnesota Hardy, Frosty, Carman, Veteran, and tender-fleshed Harmony.
- A U.S. Department of Agriculture (USDA) study reports that top scorers in taste are Coronet, Raritan Rose, Redglobe, Loring, Suncrest, Madison, J. H. Hale, Jefferson, Jersey Queen, Halberta Giant, Belle of Georgia, and Rio Oso Gem.

2. Soak peaches in ice water for twenty to thirty minutes before peeling. The peels waterproof the flesh, so it doesn't become waterlogged.

Keeping the Color

Fresh peaches will keep their fresh color longer if you toss them with lemon juice. If you don't want a lemony flavor, toss the peaches with a citric-acid solution that you can make yourself by combining one teaspoon of powdered citric acid with two-thirds cup of water.

Blushing Peaches and Cheese

makes 1½ cups

Serve with raw vegetables, crackers, crusty French bread, or stuffed into celery.

8 ounces cream cheese, softened
2 tablespoons grated sharp cheddar cheese
½ cup finely chopped peeled peaches (about 1 medium-size peach)
1 tablespoon minced fresh chives
½ teaspoon Dijon mustard
⅛ teaspoon paprika
1 tablespoon chopped roasted walnuts

Combine all ingredients in a small bowl and mix well. Chill.

Don't Throw Out Those Peach Peels!

Instead, make peach vinegar. Simply pile the peels into a saucepan and add white vinegar to cover. Bring to a boil, then simmer gently for about 20 minutes. Let the mixture cool, strain, bottle, and store, refrigerated.

Use peach vinegar in salad dressings, marinades, and sauces. Or mix a bit with plain yogurt and freshly grated nutmeg and use it to dress chicken salad.

tip

Three Quick Peach Appetizers

1. Quarter peaches and re-move pits. Toss the quar-ters in lemon juice, honey, and Dijon mustard until all of the quarters have been coated. Skewer the quar-ters and grill or broil them for 1 or 2 minutes on each side. Serve on crusty bread.

2. Dot fresh peach slices with a bit of prepared horserad-ish and wrap with a strip of lightly smoked fish.

3. Spark up shrimp cocktail by adding fresh peach slices. Serve with cocktail sauce to which a bit of grated orange peel has been added.

Peach Salad with Walnut Vinaigrette

4 servings

Dressing:
3 tablespoons walnut oil
3 tablespoons white wine vinegar

Salad:
1 Belgian endive
4 large ripe peaches, peeled, pitted, and sliced
1 tablespoon minced red onions
3 tablespoons slivered walnuts, toasted
  few sprigs of watercress for garnish

To prepare the dressing: In a small bowl, slowly whisk oil into vinegar, whisking until emulsified. Set aside.

To prepare the salad: On a chilled serving plate, arrange endive leaves in a spoke pattern. Arrange peach slices on endive. Sprinkle with onions and walnuts. Garnish with watercress sprigs. Just before serving, spoon dressing over salad.

Variation: Substitute spinach, escarole, endive, or lettuce leaves for Belgian endive.

Icehouse Peach Soup

4 servings

4 large ripe peaches, peeled, pitted, and cut into chunks
1 tablespoon fresh lemon juice
2 cardamom seeds
2 coriander seeds
4 teaspoons fresh orange juice
½ teaspoon finely grated orange peel
1½ cups buttermilk

Puree peaches with lemon juice in a food processor or blender until smooth. Pour into a medium-size bowl.

With a mortar and pestle, thoroughly crush together cardamom and coriander. Add to peach puree along with remaining ingredients. Stir until well combined. Chill thoroughly for at least 3 hours or overnight.

Note: If peaches are not especially flavorful, add honey to taste.

Ideas for Peach Salads

Slice fresh peaches and toss them with:

- almonds, raisins, endive, minced fresh ginger, and white wine vinegar
- watercress, minced scallions, walnuts, lemon juice, and a splash of walnut oil
- roasted peanuts, red onions, leaf lettuce, apple cider vinegar, and a bit of freshly grated orange peel
- celery, yogurt, and grated lime peel
- shredded cooked chicken, chives, plain yogurt, and a dash of curry powder
- spinach, thinly sliced radishes, butter lettuce, lemon juice, and ground allspice

Easy Peach Desserts

Toss fresh peach slices with:

- yogurt, cherries, and almond extract
- raspberries, freshly grated nutmeg, and orange juice
- blueberries, ground cardamom, grated orange peel, and ground cinnamon
- bananas, lemon juice, and sesame seeds
- toasted pine nuts, orange sections, and dried currants
- maple syrup, lemon juice, and pecans
- dried apricots and freshly grated ginger
- minced prunes, minced fresh mint, and apple juice

Peach-Stuffed Cornish Game Hen

4 servings

Rich and fragrant with an aura of India.

Marinade:
   1 large peach, peeled, pitted, and cut into chunks
   1 cup apple juice
   ½ teaspoon freshly crushed star anise (about 2 stars)
   ½ teaspoon freshly ground cardamom (seeds of 3 pods)
   ½ teaspoon ground ginger
   5 black peppercorns
   2 teaspoons soy sauce

   4 cornish game hens

Stuffing:
   ½ cup dried wild rice
1½ cups chicken stock
   1 bay leaf
   ⅓ cup onions
   ½ cup chopped peaches
   2 tablespoons coarsely chopped pine nuts

To prepare the marinade: In a food processor or blender, puree peaches until smooth (you should have about ½ cup).

In a large, deep dish, combine juice, puree, anise, cardamom, ginger, peppercorns, and soy sauce.

Add hens, cover, and let marinate in the refrigerator overnight.

On the following day, remove hens from marinade and set aside, reserving marinade.

To prepare the stuffing: In a medium-size saucepan, combine rice, stock, and bay leaf. Cook as you would for other rices, except increase the cooking time. Set aside.

In a medium-size saucepan, warm 1 tablespoon of the marinade. Add onions and cook until wilted, adding more marinade, if necessary. Add peaches, pine nuts, and wild rice, and heat through, adding marinade if mixture becomes too dry.

Remove bay leaf from stuffing. Fill cavities of hens with equal portions of stuffing and set in a lightly oiled 13 × 9-inch baking pan. Bake in a preheated 350°F oven for about 1 hour, basting occasionally with marinade. If hens appear to be getting too brown, cover with foil.

Peaches for Breakfast and Brunch

- Chop fresh peaches and add them to pancake and waffle batter before cooking.
- Add texture and flavor to hot cereals by stirring in chopped fresh peaches about a minute before the cereal has finished cooking.
- Substitute one-third of the liquid in pancake, waffle, and French toast recipes with peach puree.
- Fill omelets and crepes with thinly sliced fresh peaches and a dash of freshly grated nutmeg.

Prawns with Peach Dipping Sauce

makes about ½ cup sauce, or enough for 1 pound of prawns

Dipping sauce is also good with chicken chunks.

2 peaches, peeled, pitted, and cut into chunks
½ teaspoon apple cider vinegar
1 teaspoon honey
1 teaspoon prepared horseradish
1 pound steamed prawns or shrimp, shelled and deveined

Puree peaches until smooth.

In a small saucepan, combine peaches, vinegar, and honey, and simmer for about 5 minutes. Add horseradish and serve warm or at room temperature with prawns or shrimp.

Frozen Whole Peaches

If you've got the room, freeze whole peaches. When you're ready to use them, pour boiling water over them for about 3 seconds and the skins will come right off. Let them defrost and use in salads or desserts.

For a delicious and frosty beverage, puree 1 peeled peach with ½ cup of apple juice.

A Peachy Garnish

Garnish chilled summer soups with fresh peaches sliced into matchstick-size pieces. They're a beautiful contrast to creamy green soups, such as watercress and zucchini.

Peach-Glazed Spareribs

4 servings

This glaze is great for chicken, too.

    3 pounds spareribs
    1 bay leaf
    1 pound peaches, peeled, pitted, and cut into chunks
    1 tablespoon honey
    ¾ teaspoon minced ginger root
    1 clove garlic, minced
    ½ teaspoon rice vinegar
      dash of cayenne pepper

If spareribs are in a rack, cut them into separate ribs. Place in a 5-quart pot. Add bay leaf and enough water to cover. Bring to a boil. Reduce heat and simmer for 5 minutes. Drain spareribs and lay them on a rack in a 14 × 10 × 2-inch roasting pan.

Puree peaches in a food processor or blender until smooth. Transfer to a saucepan and bring to a boil. Simmer for 30 minutes. Stir in honey, ginger, garlic, vinegar, and cayenne.

Preheat oven to 350°F.

Roast ribs for 20 minutes. Brush with peach mixture and continue roasting for another 20 minutes, brushing frequently with peach mixture and turning ribs occasionally.

Serve with warmed remaining glaze, if desired.

Frozen Peach Yogurt

makes about 4 cups

    2 cups chopped peeled peaches
    2 cups plain yogurt
    ⅓ to ½ cup honey
    1 teaspoon vanilla extract
    ½ teaspoon pumpkin pie spice

Combine all ingredients in a food processor or blender and puree until smooth. Pour mixture into an ice cream maker and process according to manufacturer's instructions.

Note: Yogurt can be prepared without an ice cream maker. Simply pour pureed mixture into an 8-inch-square glass dish, cover, and freeze. Puree briefly in a food processor or blender before serving.

tip

Peach Puree to Freeze

Cook 1 cup of peeled, pureed peaches with 1 tablespoon of lemon juice for about 5 minutes. Let the puree cool, then freeze it. Defrost and use in soups, sauces, marinades, and for baking.

Peach and Apricot Bars

makes about 20 bars

2 tablespoons honey
1⅔ cups whole wheat pastry flour, divided
⅓ cup butter, softened
¾ cup dried apricots, divided
½ teaspoon baking powder
2 eggs, beaten
¼ cup honey
¾ cup milk
1 cup shredded unsweetened coconut, divided
1 cup peach jam

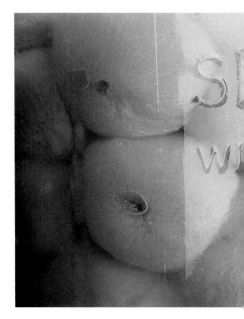

Preheat oven to 350°F. Butter a 9-inch-square baking pan.

Combine honey and 1 cup of the flour in a medium-size bowl. Cut in butter with a pastry blender until mixture looks like coarse crumbs.

Press crumbs evenly into bottom of baking pan. Bake for 25 minutes, or until lightly golden. Remove and cool slightly on a wire rack.

Finely chop ½ cup of dried apricots. Combine chopped apricots with the remaining flour, baking powder, eggs, honey, milk, and ½ cup of the coconut. Spread evenly over bottom crust. Return pan to oven and bake for 30 to 35 minutes.

Remove from oven and let cool slightly. Spread with peach jam and sprinkle with remaining coconut. Cool and cut into bars. Chop the remaining apricots into pieces, placing a piece on each bar.

tip

Honey-Peach Freeze

Chop peeled and pitted peaches. Add a bit of honey to taste, and freeze the mixture in soup cans or similar containers. Turn out the frozen peaches, slice, and serve with vanilla ice cream and gingersnaps.

Peach and Lemon Cream Tart

8 to 10 servings

Pastry:
  ½ cup butter
  1 cup whole wheat pastry flour
  1 cup unbleached white flour
  5 or 6 tablespoons cold water

Filling:
  ¾ cup honey
1¾ cups water
  ¼ cup cornstarch
  4 egg yolks
  ½ cup lemon juice
  3 tablespoons butter
  ½ cup plain yogurt
  ½ teaspoon lemon peel

Topping:
  2 cups sliced peeled peaches (about 3 medium-size)
  ½ cup apricot or peach preserves
1½ teaspoons unflavored gelatin
  2 tablespoons water or fruit juice

To prepare the pastry: In a medium-size mixing bowl, cut butter into whole wheat flour and white flour until butter is size of small peas. Make a well in the flour and add water gradually. Mix water into the flour in a circular motion. Dough should be soft enough to gather into a ball, but not sticky. Refrigerate dough for at least 2 hours or longer.

When ready to roll out, place dough between 2 sheets of plastic wrap or waxed paper. Roll to about a ⅛-inch thickness. Remove top paper from dough and place dough over tart pan. Remove bottom sheet of paper and fit dough into pan, trimming edges. Prick dough with a fork and weight bottom with pie weights. Preheat oven to 450°F and bake shell for about 12 minutes, or until lightly browned. Let cool before filling.

To prepare the filling: Combine honey, water, and cornstarch in top of a double boiler set over boiling water and placed over medium-high heat. Whisk constantly until thickened. Remove from heat. Cool slightly.

In a small bowl, beat egg yolks. Then slowly add about ¼ cup of the warm cornstarch mixture to egg yolks, stirring constantly. Add egg yolks back to cornstarch mixture and return to heat. Heat slowly until mixture bubbles and thickens. Remove from heat and stir in lemon juice and butter. Cool. While mixture is cooling, combine yogurt and lemon peel. Gently fold yogurt into lemon filling. Pour into baked pie shell.

To prepare the topping: Arrange peaches in a circular pattern over lemon cream filling. Heat apricot or peach preserves over medium heat until melted. Strain preserves through a strainer. Return strained preserves to saucepan, add gelatin and water or fruit juice, and stir over medium heat until dissolved. Bring mixture to a boil for 30 seconds. Remove from heat. When cooled slightly, glaze peaches with a pastry brush.

CHAPTER 16

PEARS

A pear is one of those fruits that looks as luscious as it tastes—all smooth, generous curves, perhaps golden yellow with a rich blush of pink. Some varieties are gently spicy; others are sweet; and all, if properly picked, make pleasurable eating. Sliced or pureed, pears are perfect with entrées, where their fine perfume balances strongly flavored meats and fish. Sliced and served with greens or spread with ricotta cheese, these aristocrats will grace any part of a meal.

INTO THE BASKET

- Pears should not be allowed to ripen on the tree, or their texture will become gritty. Harvest pears when the dark skin just begins to fade to yellow.
- Scars and surface blemishes do not affect fruit quality.
- Pick pears by holding a pear in your hand while giving a gentle lift to the stem.

INDOOR RIPENING AND STORAGE

- Pears ripen at room temperature and are well suited to fruit ripeners. If you don't have one, use a plastic or brown bag and leave it open a bit. Be sure to group pears together because they give off gases that help each other ripen. (Note: Anjou pears ripen normally at a chilly 32° to 50°F.)
- Pears ripen from the inside out and should not be allowed to get so ripe that they're soft on the outside, or they'll be mushy and tasteless. Pears are ready when the neck of the fruit is firm (not hard) to the touch, the flesh is responsive to gentle pressure, and their aromatic quality has increased.
- When ripe, pears should be eaten immediately or stored in the refrigerator or another cold, moist place for several days.
- Pears used for cooking, baking, and canning should be slightly underripe and very firm to the touch.
- To store pears, take them directly from the tree to a temperature of about 32°F and humidity of about 85 percent. Pears will last two to six months, depending on the variety.

Weights and Measures

2 pounds pears
 = 6 Anjou
 = 7 Bartlett
 = 5 Bosc
 = 5 Comice
 = 7 or 8 Devoe
 = 15 to 17 Seckel
6 medium-large pears, sliced
 = 5 cups
1 medium-large pear, cut
into 1-inch cubes
 = 1¼ cups
2 medium-large pears, diced
 = 1½ cups
1 medium-large pear, cut
into julienne strips
 = 1¼ cups

- Never store pears near potatoes, or the pears will pick up an objectionably earthy odor.

CULINARY TECHNIQUES

Perfect Peeled Pears

Depending on the variety and your personal taste, pears for canning, cooking, and baking can be peeled. Remember that the pears for these uses should be slightly underripe and very firm to the touch. Using a slotted spoon or ladle, dip a pear in and out of boiling water. When cool enough to handle, the peel and brown-green layer underneath can be easily removed with a sharp knife.

Fast Slices

Use an apple slicer with eight to twelve sections to quickly core and slice pears.

Keep Those Slices White

Toss pear slices with lime, orange, or grapefruit juice to keep them from turning brown. Lemon juice is too strong and will mask the delicate flavor of pears.

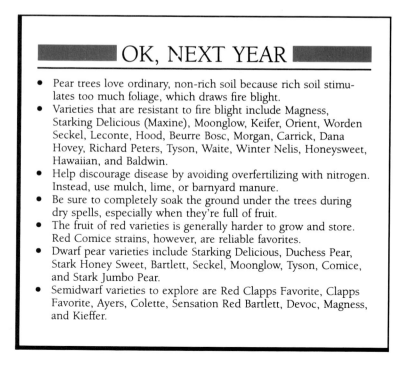

OK, NEXT YEAR

- Pear trees love ordinary, non-rich soil because rich soil stimulates too much foliage, which draws fire blight.
- Varieties that are resistant to fire blight include Magness, Starking Delicious (Maxine), Moonglow, Keifer, Orient, Worden Seckel, Leconte, Hood, Beurre Bosc, Morgan, Carrick, Dana Hovey, Richard Peters, Tyson, Waite, Winter Nelis, Honeysweet, Hawaiian, and Baldwin.
- Help discourage disease by avoiding overfertilizing with nitrogen. Instead, use mulch, lime, or barnyard manure.
- Be sure to completely soak the ground under the trees during dry spells, especially when they're full of fruit.
- The fruit of red varieties is generally harder to grow and store. Red Comice strains, however, are reliable favorites.
- Dwarf pear varieties include Starking Delicious, Duchess Pear, Stark Honey Sweet, Bartlett, Seckel, Moonglow, Tyson, Comice, and Stark Jumbo Pear.
- Semidwarf varieties to explore are Red Clapps Favorite, Clapps Favorite, Ayers, Colette, Sensation Red Bartlett, Devoc, Magness, and Kieffer.

Pears on the Half Shell

4 servings

Anjou pears are perfect here, but any other ripe variety will work.

¼ cup plain yogurt
¼ cup mayonnaise
1 teaspoon Dijon mustard
2 tablespoons minced fresh parsley
1 tablespoon minced fresh chives
1 teaspoon minced fresh chervil
1½ cups crabmeat
½ cup chopped celery
1 small tomato, seeded and chopped
4 pears
mixed salad greens

In a small bowl, combine yogurt, mayonnaise, mustard, parsley, chives, and chervil.

In another bowl, combine crabmeat, celery, and tomato. Pour dressing over mixture and toss gently to combine. Chill for 1 or 2 hours.

Place pears into a colander. Pour boiling water over them for 5 or 6 seconds. Let cool. Cut pears into halves and core, using a melon baller or a small spoon.

Fill each pear cavity with some crabmeat mixture. Place pear halves on salad greens to serve.

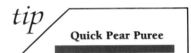

Quick Pear Puree

Peel and coarsely chop ripe pears. Toss with lemon, lime, or orange juice. Puree in a food processor or blender until smooth. Turn into freezer containers and store in freezer. Although it will darken slightly, the defrosted puree can be used in dessert breads and cakes. For a quick pear sauce, heat puree and add cinnamon.

Speedy Pear Appetizers

- Halve pears, remove cores, and toss in orange juice. Fill centers with sharp cheese, chopped walnuts, and a dash of freshly grated nutmeg. Broil briefly and serve warm.
- Chop pears and combine with cooked baby shrimp, minced scallions, and diced celery. Toss with yogurt, curry powder, and ground ginger. Serve in crisp lettuce shells.
- Create an easy filling for crepes by combining chopped pears, dried currants, nutmeg, pear juice, and a bit of cornstarch. Cook to thicken.
- Build canapés by starting with a thin slice of French bread coated with a bit of mustard. Place a thin slice of chicken over the mustard and top with a thin slice of pear and a sprig of dill.

Icy Pear Soup

6 to 8 servings

Anjou pears are wonderful in this recipe.

2 tablespoons butter
2 leeks (white part plus 1 inch of light green), sliced
½ cup chopped celery
1 medium-size potato, diced
3 cups chicken stock
  freshly ground white pepper to taste
3 large pears, peeled and chopped
2 cups cold milk
  freshly grated nutmeg to taste

In a large saucepan, melt butter over low heat. Add leeks and celery and sauté for 5 minutes, or until soft. Add potatoes, stock, and pepper. Bring to a boil. Reduce heat and simmer for 25 to 30 minutes, or until vegetables are soft. Cool slightly. Carefully puree in a food processor or blender until smooth. Add pears and puree. Pour into a large bowl. Stir in milk and nutmeg. Chill thoroughly, at least 2 hours.

Pears Baked with Swordfish

4 servings

1 pound swordfish, cut into 4 pieces
1 red onion, cut into thin rings
1 pound pears, peeled and cut into julienne strips
1 teaspoon minced ginger root
  dash of grated lime peel
  juice of 2 limes
2 whole allspice berries, crushed

Preheat oven to 500°F.
Set each piece of fish on a square of aluminum foil that's big enough to fold over and enclose fish. Place one-quarter of the onion rings, pears, ginger, lime peel, lime juice, and allspice on each piece of fish. Fold foil around each to make a tight pack and bake for 15 minutes.

Pears Stuffed with Sausage and Fennel

6 servings

½ pound lean sausage
2 tablespoons finely minced onions
¼ cup minced fresh mushrooms
1 teaspoon fennel seeds, thoroughly crushed
½ teaspoon minced fresh rosemary or ⅛ teaspoon
     crumbled dried rosemary
  freshly ground black pepper to taste
1 cup fine whole grain bread crumbs, made from
     day-old French bread
6 large red Bartlett pears

If sausage is coarse, put through a food processor or grinder until fine.

In a nonstick skillet, cook sausage and onions together over medium-low heat until sausage is cooked and onions are soft, about 10 minutes. Add mushrooms and cook for 3 or 4 minutes. Add fennel, rosemary, pepper, and bread crumbs, and combine thoroughly. Remove from heat and set aside.

Cut off about 1 inch from the top of each pear. Using a melon baller or small spoon, remove pulp and core, leaving a ½- to ¾-inch shell. Stuff each pear with sausage mixture. Chill pears.

Immediately before serving, cut each pear into ½-inch slices. Arrange attractively on a serving plate.

What's an Asian Pear?

An Asian pear is a crisp, applelike, juicy, refreshing, crunchy pear. Asian pears ripen on the tree and are so sturdy that they will last for a week or two at room temperature or for three months in the refrigerator.

Eat them raw, poached, in salads, or exactly as you would apples. In fact, experts say if you can grow apples, you can grow Asian pears.

Pear Salad Ideas

- chopped pears, julienned carrots, freshly ground allspice, lemon zest, and yogurt
- sliced pears, chopped coconut, shredded lettuce, lime juice, and peanut oil
- slivered pears, tossed with cooked rice, minced shallots, sliced mushrooms, watercress, and chopped pecans
- chopped pears, steamed scallops, diced water chestnuts, shredded spinach, minced ginger root, and lemon juice
- chopped pears, shredded chicken, tangerine sections, tarragon, orange juice, and white wine vinegar

Scallops of Veal
with Green and Red Pears

4 servings

¼ cup whole wheat flour
⅛ teaspoon freshly grated nutmeg
⅛ teaspoon freshly ground white pepper
 1 pound veal scallops (¼ inch thick), lightly pounded
 2 teaspoons olive oil
 1 cup plus 3 tablespoons chicken stock, divided
 2 medium-size shallots, minced
 3 red and green unpeeled Bartlett pears, thinly sliced
½ teaspoon Dijon mustard
⅛ teaspoon crumbled fresh savory
 1 tablespoon minced fresh parsley
   freshly ground black pepper to taste

Combine flour, nutmeg, and white pepper in a shallow dish. Dredge veal scallops in mixture, shaking off excess.

In a large nonstick skillet, heat oil over medium-high heat. Sauté scallops, 3 at a time, about 1½ minutes per side, or until golden. Transfer to an ovenproof platter. Cover with aluminum foil and keep warm in a low oven.

Add 3 tablespoons of the stock to the skillet. Add shallots and sauté for 3 minutes, or until soft, stirring frequently. Add pears and cook for 3 or 4 minutes, or until soft, stirring gently. Remove pears with a slotted spoon and keep warm.

Add remaining stock to the skillet, increase heat, and boil until liquid is reduced by half. Stir in mustard, savory, parsley, and black pepper.

To serve, arrange veal and pears attractively on a warm serving dish and surround with sauce.

The Old Pear-in-the-Bottle Trick

Did you ever wonder who puts the pears in those bottles of brandy and how they do it? Nowadays, it's often done through the bottom of the bottle, which is attached after the pear and brandy are inside. The feat used to be engineered by tying empty bottles onto bud-bearing branches. When the fruit was mature, the stem was snipped and the bottle filled with brandy.

If you have pear brandy, be sure to refill continually so that the pear remains covered. It will spoil if you don't.

Pear and Barley Stuffing

6 servings

      1 to 1½ pounds pears, peeled and chopped
1¼ cups chicken stock
  2 medium-size shallots, minced
  1 cup milk
½ teaspoon dry mustard
¼ teaspoon dried thyme
     dash of ground nutmeg
  2 cups cooked barley

In a food processor, puree pears and juice until smooth. (You should have about 1 cup puree.)

In a medium-size skillet, bring stock to a boil. Add shallots and cook over medium-high heat until liquid is reduced to about ¼ cup, about 10 minutes. Reduce heat to low and add pear puree and milk. Cook, stirring frequently, until mixture is thick and smooth and has been reduced by half, about 5 minutes. Remove from heat and stir in mustard, thyme, nutmeg, and barley.

Use to stuff a 3½- to 4-pound roasting chicken or 6 large boneless chicken breasts.

Spiced Pears

tip

Spiced Pears

Slice a pound of pears and add them to a saucepan with ½ cup of apple or pear juice. Toss in ½ cup of sliced onions, 3 bay leaves, 3 crushed allspice berries, and a cinnamon stick. Poach the pears for 30 minutes and serve with roasted poultry and meats.

Dutch Pear Cake

10 to 12 servings

½ cup plus 1 tablespoon chopped walnuts, divided
1 teaspoon ground cinnamon
½ cup date sugar
½ cup plus 1 tablespoon butter, divided
½ cup plus 2 tablespoons honey, divided
1 cup plain yogurt
1 teaspoon vanilla extract
2 eggs
1¼ cups whole wheat pastry flour
1¼ cups unbleached white flour
1 teaspoon baking soda
1 teaspoon baking powder
3 medium-size pears, peeled and sliced
1 tablespoon chopped walnuts

Preheat oven to 325°F.

In a small mixing bowl, combine ½ cup of the walnuts, cinnamon, and date sugar. Set aside.

In a large mixing bowl, cream together ½ cup of the butter and ½ cup of the honey. Add yogurt and beat in. Add vanilla and eggs and beat in.

In a medium-size bowl, sift whole wheat flour, white flour, baking soda, and baking powder. Stir flour mixture into butter mixture until well combined. Beat batter for 3 minutes, scraping bowl occasionally with a spatula.

Pour half the batter into a 12-cup Bundt pan sprayed with vegetable spray. Sprinkle with nut mixture and layer sliced pears. Cover pears and nut mixture with remaining batter.

Bake for 35 to 40 minutes, or until cake tester comes out clean. Let cool for 10 minutes and then turn out onto a wire rack. While cake is cooling, warm the remaining butter and remaining honey together in a small saucepan. When well combined, pour over cake and sprinkle with the remaining walnuts.

Polar Pears

Unblanched pear slices freeze beautifully. Simply slice pears and toss recipe-size portions into freezer bags or containers and freeze. They'll last for about three months.

Use the slices (no need to defrost) in tarts, cakes, pies, or stewed fruit recipes. Or you may warm them, add spices, and serve with roasted meats and poultry.

Pear and Apricot Strudel

8 to 10 servings

¼ cup walnut pieces
½ cup dried apricots
2½ cups peeled and sliced pears
¼ teaspoon ground cinnamon
¼ teaspoon ground nutmeg
1 tablespoon lemon juice
⅓ cup maple syrup
8 phyllo dough sheets
3 to 4 tablespoons butter, melted

Preheat oven to 350°F.

Grind walnut pieces finely. Reserve.

Place apricots in a small saucepan with enough water to cover. Simmer for 15 minutes. Drain.

Coarsely chop apricots and place in a medium-size mixing bowl with pears, cinnamon, and nutmeg. Add lemon juice and maple syrup, and combine thoroughly. Set aside.

Lay phyllo sheets flat and cover with a damp towel to prevent them from drying out. Lay 1 sheet of phyllo on counter and brush lightly with butter. Cover with another sheet of phyllo and brush lightly again with butter. Repeat this procedure until all 8 leaves have been used. Sprinkle phyllo with reserved walnuts. Place pear mixture on lower half of long side of dough, leaving an inch on the bottom and ½ inch on both sides. Fold sides over filling and brush lightly with butter. Fold bottom over filling, and then roll strudel. Brush with remaining butter and place seam-side down on a lightly buttered baking sheet. Bake for 35 minutes, or until golden.

CHAPTER 17

RASPBERRIES

Like sips of an elegant wine, raspberries are best appreciated when eaten by themselves. But raspberries, of course, do well with classic dessert flavors like nuts, vanilla, lemon, lime, orange, mint, and cream, and they're famous in tarts, tortes, crepes, and sauces. But don't stop there. Toss them gently into a salad with avocado and lobster chunks or with poached chicken, oranges, and butter lettuce, drizzled with raspberry vinegar. Use them as an edible garnish for roast poultry, grilled or sautéed fish, chilled fruit soups, or rice pilaf.

INTO THE BASKET

Use a gentle hand when picking raspberries. Place two or three fingers on the berry and gently slip it from its core. If it doesn't budge easily, don't force it. Instead, check it again the next day. Set the picked berries into small, shallow containers, so they won't crush, and keep the containers in the shade during picking.

INDOOR STORAGE

- Store raspberries, unwashed and uncovered, in the refrigerator, and they'll keep for about two days.
- Crushed or damaged berries should be kept separately from whole ones and used at once.

CULINARY TECHNIQUES

Cleaning

Raspberries are delicate and, if you know they have been grown organically, shouldn't be washed at all before you use them. Simply pick out the pieces of leaf and twig by hand.

Seeding

The easiest way to seed raspberries is to press berries through a wire mesh strainer with the back of a large spoon.

Weights and Measures

1 pint raspberries
   = ½ pound
   = 3½ cups
1 pint raspberries, pressed
through a sieve
   = 2 cups
1 pint raspberries, pureed in
a food processor
   = 2½ cups
1 pint raspberries, pureed in
a food processor and then
pressed through a sieve
   = 2 cups

▨▨▨ OK, NEXT YEAR ▨▨▨

- Of all raspberries, red raspberries are the easiest to grow. Heritage is popular in northern climates and Dormanred and Southland are favored in the South.
- Purple varieties are the second easiest to grow. Try Purple Royalty, Brandywine, Clyde, Amethyst, and Sodus.
- Black raspberries are more difficult to grow than red or purple, but Lowden Black, Cumberland, Jewel, Bristol, Black Treasure, and Allen are favorite varieties.
- Yellow varieties are the most susceptible of all to disease, but their flavor is delicious. Fall Gold and Amber are varieties to try.
- Fairview and Willamette are good western-growing varieties.
- One-crop varieties include Newburgh (red), Taylor (red), Hilton (red), Latham (red), Brandywine (purple), and Jewel (black).
- Two-crop everbearers to try are Heritage (red), Fall Gold (yellow), and Black Treasure (black).
- Milton is a red variety that freezes particularly well.
- One way to fight raspberry diseases is to transplant every year, reports Doug Campbell of the Raspberry Testing Group of the North American Fruit Explorers. Transplanting can be done in the spring, as soon as the ground is soft or in the fall after the first killing frost.

Raspberry-Pecan Dressing

makes about ½ cup

Great served over cooked shredded poultry or over potato, pasta, or green salads.

   2 tablespoons white wine vinegar
   1 tablespoon walnut oil
      pinch of dry mustard
   ½ cup raspberries
   2 tablespoons chopped pecans

   In a medium-size bowl, whisk together vinegar, oil, and mustard. Add raspberries and crush them with a potato masher. Stir in pecans and serve at room temperature or chilled.

Raspberry Salad Ideas

- black raspberries, sliced pears, avocado, and watercress with orange vinaigrette
- red raspberries, chopped artichoke hearts, fresh spinach, sliced red onions, lemon juice, and a splash of olive oil
- whole raspberries, cooked shrimp, cooked crab, and fresh tarragon, drizzled with champagne or sherry vinegar
- whole raspberries, asparagus tips, fresh chervil, and sorrel, tossed with a clear vinaigrette
- whole raspberries, shredded cooked chicken, and fresh rosemary, served on alfalfa sprouts with orange-flavored yogurt on the side
- whole raspberries, pineapple chunks, orange sections, and fresh mint, served in a pineapple half
- whole red and black raspberries, tossed gently into cooked cracked wheat and dressed with lemon juice, fresh thyme, and a splash of olive oil

Chilled Blackcap Soup

8 servings

4 cups black raspberries
4 cups water
½ cup fresh, strained orange juice
1 tablespoon lemon juice
1 3-inch stick cinnamon
⅓ cup honey, or to taste
   plain yogurt or sour cream
   finely grated orange rind or thyme sprigs for garnish

Combine raspberries, water, juices, cinnamon stick, and honey in a 3-quart saucepan. Bring to a boil. Lower heat and simmer for 10 minutes. Pour through a sieve to remove seeds. Cover and chill thoroughly, at least 3 hours.

Ladle into individual serving bowls. Top each serving with a bit of yogurt or sour cream and a sprinkling of orange rind or a thyme sprig.

Variation: Substitute red raspberries for black raspberries.

Sauté of Sole with Raspberries

4 servings

      1 pound sole or flounder fillets
   1½ tablespoons whole wheat flour
      1 teaspoon butter
      1 teaspoon olive oil
      ¼ cup raspberry vinegar or other fruited vinegar
      ¼ cup chicken stock
         pinch of dried tarragon
         pinch of freshly grated orange peel
      1 cup raspberries

   Sprinkle fish with flour while you warm butter and oil in a skillet. Add fish and sauté for about 1½ minutes on each side, or until fish has become golden in places. Remove fish to a heated platter.
   Add vinegar and stock to skillet and boil, using a spatula to scrape pieces off bottom of pan. When sauce has been reduced by half, toss in tarragon, orange peel, and raspberries, and remove from heat. Pour sauce over fish and serve immediately.

Stuffed Steamed Chicken in a Raspberry Mirror

serves 6 to 8 as an appetizer or 4 as a light entrée

The mirror is merely a shiny raspberry puree.

Chicken:
   1 pound boneless, skinless chicken breasts, cut into 4 pieces
      about 12 large spinach leaves
   ¼ cup shredded Havarti cheese or other mild white cheese
   2 scallions, minced

Mirror:
1½ cups raspberries (not white or golden)
   ¼ teaspoon Dijon mustard

Stuffed Steamed Chicken in a Raspberry Mirror

To prepare the chicken: Set water to boil in bottom of a steamer.

Sandwich each piece of chicken between 2 pieces of waxed paper and gently pound with a mallet until about ¼ inch thick.

Set a piece of chicken horizontally in front of you on a piece of plastic wrap. Cover chicken with 3 spinach leaves, tearing them to fit, if necessary. Then sprinkle on one-quarter of the cheese and one-quarter of the scallions. From the side closest to you, roll chicken jelly-roll style, using plastic wrap to nudge it along. Roll plastic wrap tightly around chicken and set roll aside while you prepare the remaining chicken rolls. Then place rolls in the steamer, cover, and steam for 15 minutes.

To prepare the mirror: Press raspberries through a wire strainer with the back of a large spoon, using a bowl underneath to catch the puree (you'll have about ½ cup of puree). Add mustard and stir to combine.

Let chicken rolls cool slightly, remove plastic wrap, and slice them into half-inch disks. The end pieces may need to be trimmed or placed so they're pretty-side up.

Pour mirror into a pool on a serving platter or individual plates and arrange chicken disks on it. Serve immediately.

tip

Raspberry Tea

Use the leaves of unsprayed raspberry plants to make herbal tea. Steep about 1 teaspoon of crumbled dried leaves in 1 cup of boiling water for about 5 minutes.

Raspberry tea combines well with lemon verbena, lemongrass, lemon balm, bergamot, and dried orange peel.

Nancy's Secret Raspberry Cake

10 to 12 servings

Cake:
½ cup whole wheat pastry flour
½ cup unbleached white flour
6 eggs, separated
½ cup honey, warmed, divided
1 teaspoon vanilla extract
⅛ teaspoon cream of tartar

Lime Curd Filling:
4 egg yolks, room temperature
¼ cup honey, warmed
¼ cup fresh, strained lime juice
1 teaspoon grated lime peel
¼ cup butter, cut into ½-inch pieces, room temperature

2 cups red or black raspberries
1 cup heavy cream (optional)
1 tablespoon honey (optional)

To prepare the cake: Preheat oven to 350°F. Butter bottom of a 9-inch springform pan. Line bottom of pan with waxed paper, then butter and flour waxed paper.

Sift whole wheat pastry flour and white flour together 3 times. Set aside.

In a large mixing bowl, beat egg yolks at high speed of an electric mixer until light and lemon-colored. Gradually beat in 6 tablespoons of the honey. Continue beating until mixture is very thick and smooth, 12 to 15 minutes. Do not underbeat, since lightness of cake depends on this step. Beat in vanilla.

In a separate bowl with clean beaters, beat egg whites until foamy. Add cream of tartar and beat until soft peaks form. Gradually beat in the remaining honey and continue to beat until stiff peaks form. Gently fold one-quarter of the egg whites into yolk mixture. Fold in the remaining whites.

Fold in flour mixture gently but thoroughly, one-third at a time. Pour batter into prepared pan and bake for 35 to 40 minutes, or until top springs back when lightly touched and cake tester comes out clean. Remove to a wire rack. Cool in pan for 10 minutes. Remove sides of pan. Invert cake onto a rack, remove bottom of pan and waxed paper. Cool cake completely.

To prepare the filling: Beat egg yolks and honey together in a small bowl. Add lime juice and peel and butter. Transfer to the top of a double boiler and set over simmering water. Heat slowly, stirring constantly, until butter melts and mixture is thick enough to coat a metal spoon. (Do not let mixture come to a boil or it will curdle.) Pour mixture through a fine strainer to remove rind. Cover lime curd with a piece of waxed paper. Place in the refrigerator and chill thoroughly. (Filling may be prepared 1 day in advance.)

To assemble the cake: Cover cake and place in the freezer for 1 hour. Remove from freezer and place on a serving dish. Cut a circle 1 inch deep, 1 inch inside cake edge. With a small serrated knife, cut horizontally to the center of the circle ¼ inch deep. Turn cake over to free the thin circle. Remove the cake under the lid by slicing into wedges to a 1-inch depth. Do not cut through bottom of cake. Remove the wedges of cake and reserve for another use.

Spread two-thirds of the lime curd over bottom of hollowed-out cake. Arrange raspberries in concentric circles over lime curd, reserving a few for garnish. Replace lid of cake. Spoon the remaining lime curd over top of cake and garnish with the reserved berries.

For an optional presentation, whip cream until soft and fluffy. Gradually beat in honey and beat until mixture holds its shape. Fold the reserved one-third of the lime curd into the whipped cream. Spread the mixture over the top and sides of the cake. Garnish with the reserved berries.

Note: Add the unused wedges of cake to your favorite bread pudding recipe.

tip

Raspberry Lemonade

Add 1 teaspoon of raspberry puree to a tall glass of chilled lemonade and enjoy.

Vanilla-Almond Mousse with Raspberry Sauce

serves 6

Mousse:
  1 envelope unflavored gelatin
  ¼ cup water
  1¼ cups milk
  ¼ cup honey
  3 eggs, separated
  ½ teaspoon almond extract
  1 teaspoon vanilla extract

Sauce:
  ½ cup red or black raspberry jam
  ½ pint red or black raspberries

To prepare the mousse: Sprinkle gelatin over water in a medium-size saucepan. Let stand to soften about 5 minutes. Add milk and honey and heat slowly. Beat egg yolks. Slowly add some of the warm milk mixture to egg yolks, whisking constantly. Add egg yolks back to warm milk mixture, stirring constantly. Stir until slightly thickened. Remove from heat, add extracts, and chill until thickened but not set, about 45 minutes.

In a small bowl, beat egg whites until stiff. Fold into chilled mixture. Pour into a 1-quart mold and refrigerate until firm, 6 hours or overnight.

To prepare the sauce: Melt jam in a small saucepan over low heat, whisking to keep smooth. When melted, remove from heat and stir in raspberries. Chill.

When ready to serve, unmold mousse on a flat serving dish. Spoon sauce over mold.

Ideas for Using Raspberries in Desserts

- gently tossed with vanilla crème fraîche
- gently tossed with chantilly cream
- atop puff pastry
- in a parfait with honey-vanilla ice cream
- atop a lemon or orange mousse
- atop pancakes, waffles, or crepes
- atop pound cake
- atop rice pudding
- atop vanilla pudding
- atop cheesecake

Raspberry Tea Bread

makes 1 loaf

  6 tablespoons butter
  ½ cup honey
  ½ teaspoon vanilla extract
  2 eggs
  1 cup whole wheat pastry flour
  ¾ cup unbleached white flour

1 teaspoon baking powder
½ teaspoon baking soda
⅓ cup plain yogurt
⅓ cup raspberry jam

Preheat oven to 350°F. Coat an 8½ × 4½-inch loaf pan with vegetable spray.

Cream butter and honey together. Add vanilla and eggs, one at a time, beating after each addition.

In another bowl, sift together whole wheat flour, white flour, baking powder, and baking soda. Add dry mixture to creamed mixture alternately with yogurt until well blended. Fold raspberry jam carefully into mixture. Turn batter into prepared loaf pan and bake for about 50 minutes, or until knife inserted in center comes out clean.

Raspberry Slush

makes about 2 cups

1 cup raspberries or ⅔ cup raspberry puree
½ cup white grape juice
½ teaspoon lime juice
1½ cups ice

Combine all ingredients in a blender and blend until well combined and slushy. Serve immediately or freeze and reblend before serving.

Raspberry Don'ts

- Don't toss whole raspberries into quick breads or cakes. Unlike other fruit, raspberries don't pick up sweetness or flavor from the surrounding batter. The pectin in raspberries also gums up the surrounding batter.
- Raspberry puree should also be avoided in baked goods because it will leave breads and cakes gummy. The puree can also turn the cake or bread purple, blue, or green, especially in the presence of alkaline ingredients like baking soda.
- Avoid using aluminum, tin, or iron with raspberries, or it could turn the berries blue.

CHAPTER 18

STRAWBERRIES

It's impossible to imagine spring and early summer without dreaming of strawberry shortcake, strawberry tarts, and strawberry ice cream. But lately, these sweet little jewels have been stepping into entrée roles and costarring with fish and poultry.

Consider plump chicken slices rolled in crushed herbs and sautéed with fragrant strawberries. It's quick, delicious, and certainly a provocative thought as you shake the snow from your boots.

INTO THE BASKET

- Strawberries are ripe when the color is full, red, and shiny.
- Harvest strawberries the day after they ripen, even if it means daily picking.
- To pick, snap the stem between your thumbnail and forefinger, taking care not to pull the berry.

INDOOR RIPENING AND STORAGE

- If you have berries with green patches, set them out on a counter in a single layer overnight. You can also set them on top of your refrigerator, covered loosely with plastic wrap. Store ripe, unwashed berries in an open paper (not plastic) bag in the refrigerator. They'll last for several days.

CULINARY TECHNIQUES

Hulling

Perfectly ripe, well-formed berries can be hulled with a strawberry huller, which is a thick, tweezerlike device. With other berries, hull with a sharp paring knife, taking care not to disturb the flesh, or tasty juice will be lost.

Weights and Measures

1 pint strawberries
  = 12 ounces unhulled
    berries
  = 12 to 30 whole
    unhulled berries,
    depending on size
  = 3¼ cups whole
    hulled berries
  = 2¼ cups sliced hulled
    berries
  = 1⅔ cups chopped
    hulled berries
  = 1⅔ cups pureed
    hulled berries
1 pound strawberries
  = 3½ cups whole
    hulled berries
  = 2⅔ cups sliced hulled
    berries
  = 2 cups chopped
    hulled berries
  = 2 cups pureed hulled
    berries
4 ounces medium-size
unhulled berries
  = 1 cup

Alpine strawberries will not need hulling because their hulls come off automatically when they're harvested.

Always hull berries *after* they're washed, or tasty juice will be lost.

Berry Clean

Forget what you ever heard to the contrary, never wash berries before storage. Instead, wash them just before serving to preserve texture and flavor. Set them gently in a strainer or colander and rinse them with a soft stream of cool water, then pat them dry.

Mashing, Smashing, and Pureeing

For a chunky texture, use a potato masher. For a smoother texture, puree strawberries in a food processor or blender.

OK, NEXT YEAR

- Strawberries are finicky growers, so be sure to check with your local state extension office to discover what variety is best for you. Recommendations will vary, often within the same state.
- Varieties that fruit all summer are called day neutral and include Brighton, Selva, Fern, Burlington, Sakuma, Tillkum, Tribute, and Tristar.
- June-bearing varieties include Earlidawn, Surecrop, Redchief, Redglow, Apollo, Guardian, Midway, Jerseybelle, Sparkle, Dunlap, Cardinal, Earliglow, and Florida Belle.
- Everbearers that fruit once in the spring and once in the fall include Tribute and Tristar.
- If taste is your highest priority, choose Midland, Fairfax, Earliglow, Redcoat, or Ozark Beauty.
- Varieties best for freezing include Suwanee, Redchief, Redglow, Surecrop, Midway, Earlibelle, Earlidawn, Earliglow, Midland, Midway, Pocahontas, Puget Beauty, and Trumpeter.
- Avoid planting strawberries where potatoes, okra, melons, eggplant, peppers, raspberries, or peaches have grown previously because the soil may contain strawberry-attacking wilt. Wilt-resistant varieties include Catskill, Surecrop, Redchief, Sun-rise, Blakemore, Delite, Earliglow, Empire, Guardian, and Hood.
- Varieties resistant to red-stele wilt include Sparkle, Guardian, Surecrop, Delite, Earliglow, Hood, Quinault, and Redchief.
- Catskill, Fletcher, and Tioga are resistant to gray mold.
- Alpine strawberries are small red or golden berries that are easy to grow and are usually started from seed. Varieties include Baron Solemacher (Perpetual Alpine), Alexandria, Rugen Improved, and Alpine Yellow Fruited.

Strawberry Cheese

makes about 1½ cups

6 ounces mascarpone* or cream cheese
1½ teaspoons toasted poppyseeds
⅓ cup finely chopped strawberries
1 whole strawberry for garnish
thyme sprig for garnish

In a small bowl, mix together cheese, poppyseeds, and chopped strawberries. Spoon into a small, decorative serving dish and garnish with whole strawberry and thyme. Serve with crudités or little squares of toast.

*Mascarpone is a soft Italian cheese and is available at specialty food stores.

Variation: Stuff Strawberry Cheese into large, hollowed-out strawberries.

Cracked Wheat
with Strawberries and Chives

4 to 6 servings

1 cup cracked wheat
2 cups boiling water
⅓ cup minced fresh chives
1 pint strawberries, quartered
1 cup plain yogurt
⅛ teaspoon ground cinnamon
2 tablespoons lightly toasted cashews, coarsely chopped

Pour cracked wheat into a medium-size bowl and cover with boiling water. Let stand for 1 hour. Drain cracked wheat by pouring through a sieve, pressing with the back of a spoon to remove moisture. Transfer cracked wheat to a bowl and stir in chives. Cover bowl with plastic wrap and chill for 1 hour.
Stir in strawberries.
In a small bowl, stir together yogurt and cinnamon until smooth. Pour over cracked wheat mixture, toss gently, and sprinkle with cashews.

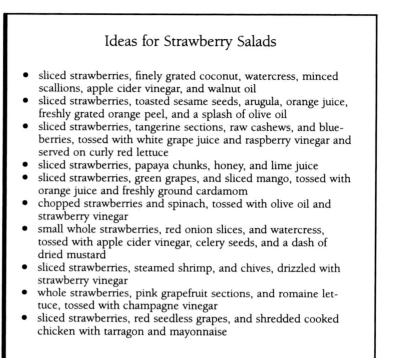

Ideas for Strawberry Salads

- sliced strawberries, finely grated coconut, watercress, minced scallions, apple cider vinegar, and walnut oil
- sliced strawberries, toasted sesame seeds, arugula, orange juice, freshly grated orange peel, and a splash of olive oil
- sliced strawberries, tangerine sections, raw cashews, and blueberries, tossed with white grape juice and raspberry vinegar and served on curly red lettuce
- sliced strawberries, papaya chunks, honey, and lime juice
- sliced strawberries, green grapes, and sliced mango, tossed with orange juice and freshly ground cardamom
- chopped strawberries and spinach, tossed with olive oil and strawberry vinegar
- small whole strawberries, red onion slices, and watercress, tossed with apple cider vinegar, celery seeds, and a dash of dried mustard
- sliced strawberries, steamed shrimp, and chives, drizzled with strawberry vinegar
- whole strawberries, pink grapefruit sections, and romaine lettuce, tossed with champagne vinegar
- sliced strawberries, red seedless grapes, and shredded cooked chicken with tarragon and mayonnaise

Strawberries, Snow Peas, and Shrimp with Raspberry Vinaigrette

4 servings

½ pound snow peas, trimmed and strings removed
1 pound cooked jumbo shrimp, peeled
1 cup frozen raspberries, thawed and drained
1 tablespoon white wine vinegar
1 tablespoon lemon juice
   freshly ground white pepper to taste
   dash of freshly grated nutmeg
3 tablespoons olive oil
1 pound strawberries, sliced

Steam peas until bright green and crisp, 45 to 60 seconds. Drain, rinse under cold water, then drain again. Put peas in a medium-size bowl, toss in shrimp, cover, and chill well.

Puree and seed raspberries by pressing them through a strainer with the back of a spoon. Transfer puree to a small bowl; whisk in vinegar, lemon juice, pepper, and nutmeg; then slowly whisk in oil.

Gently mix strawberries with snow peas and shrimp, pour on dressing, and toss.

Variations:

Add chopped red onions, chopped nuts, or sesame seeds.

Use sugar snap peas instead of snow peas. (You don't have to steam the snap peas.)

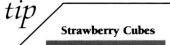

Strawberry Cubes

Fill an ice cube tray halfway with water or juice and freeze. When frozen, set a small strawberry or strawberry slice on each cube. Fill the cubes the rest of the way with water or juice. When frozen, toss the cubes into refreshing summer beverages.

Grilled Swordfish with Strawberry Marinade

4 servings

2 cups strawberries, quartered
½ cup Strawberry and Ginger Vinegar (page 203)
2 whole allspice berries
2 whole cloves
3 black peppercorns
¼ cup olive oil
2 pounds swordfish steaks, about 1 inch thick

In a small saucepan, combine strawberries and vinegar. Using a mortar and pestle, lightly crush together allspice, cloves, and peppercorns, and add to saucepan. Bring to a boil over medium heat and continue to boil for 3 minutes. Remove from heat, stir in oil, and cool to room temperature.

Arrange swordfish steaks in a shallow dish just large enough to hold them in a single layer. Pour marinade over fish. Cover dish with plastic wrap and marinate in the refrigerator for 1 hour, turning once.

Grill fish over hot coals for about 10 minutes, turning once with a wide spatula and brushing with marinade. You may also broil the fish, 2 to 4 inches from the heat source, for 5 minutes on each side.

tip

Strawberries Tempura

Create an unusual appetizer by making Strawberries Tempura, using 1 cup of whole strawberries.

In a medium-size skillet, heat 1 inch of vegetable oil to 370°F or until a drop of water sizzles when it's dropped into the oil.

Beat 2 egg whites until stiff.

In a large bowl, beat 2 egg yolks with ⅓ cup of cold water until combined. Fold in ¼ cup each of whole wheat flour and unbleached white flour, a dash of ground ginger, and egg whites.

Dip strawberries into batter until evenly coated and fry in oil until lightly browned, about 2 minutes, turning once with tongs. Do not crowd strawberries in skillet. Drain on paper towels.

Serve with applesauce, vanilla yogurt, and fresh orange sections.

Roast Veal with Strawberry Glaze

8 to 10 servings

Glaze:
　½ cup honey
　3 tablespoons water
　2 strips (½ × 2 inches) lime peel
　⅛ teaspoon ground ginger
　　dash of ground nutmeg
1½ cups sliced strawberries

Veal:
　1 loin of veal, boned and tied (4 to 4½ pounds boned meat)
　　freshly ground black pepper to taste
　1 tablespoon olive oil
　1 tablespoon butter
　2 cloves garlic, crushed
　2 large shallots, chopped
　3 sprigs thyme
　½ cup chicken stock, if necessary

To prepare the glaze: In a small saucepan, combine honey, water, and lime peel. Bring to a boil over medium heat and boil for 10 minutes. Add ginger, nutmeg, and strawberries, and continue to boil for 2 minutes. Remove from heat and cool slightly. Transfer to a food processor or blender and process until smooth. Pour back into saucepan and heat until mixture becomes clear, stirring frequently.

To prepare the veal: Preheat oven to 475°F.

Wipe veal with paper towels, rub with pepper, and brush with glaze.

Place oil and butter in a shallow, ovenproof dish and heat in the oven until very hot. Place veal in dish and sear in the oven for 10 minutes, or until brown, turning frequently. Reduce oven temperature to 350°F. Add garlic, shallots, and thyme to dish. Bake for 1¾ hours or until veal is well browned and juice is pale yellow, not pink, when meat is pierced with a small knife. Turn roast occasionally and brush often with glaze. Add stock if pan seems to be drying out on bottom.

Turn oven off and let roast sit in oven for 10 minutes. Remove meat to a carving board and thinly slice on the diagonal.

Roast Veal with Strawberry Glaze

Strawberry and Ginger Vinegar

makes about 2½ cups

Great to use in salad dressings, marinades, sauces, or sparkling water with a twist of orange.

   2 cups strawberries, halved
   2 small slices ginger root
   1 bay leaf
2½ cups white wine vinegar

     Toss strawberries, ginger, and bay leaf into a glass jar and set aside.
     In a small saucepan, heat vinegar, but don't boil. Then pour vinegar into glass jar. Cover jar and leave it, unrefrigerated, overnight.
     Drain vinegar and store in refrigerator.

Healthful Berries

Compare equal amounts of strawberries to oranges, and you will find 18 percent more vitamin C in the strawberries. Try it with grapefruits, and strawberries will show 55 percent more. And what's more, one cup of strawberries has about 60 calories.

Strawberry Mayonnaise

makes about 1¼ cups

Use as a dressing for fruit, poultry, fish, or shellfish salads.

1 egg, room temperature
½ teaspoon dry mustard
⅛ teaspoon freshly ground white pepper
2 tablespoons strained fresh lemon juice
1 cup safflower oil, divided
6 ounces strawberries

Rinse out a blender container with warm water and drain well.

Put egg, mustard, pepper, lemon juice, and ¼ cup of the oil into blender container. Cover and blend for 1 minute. Remove feeder cap and with the motor running, slowly pour in the rest of the oil in a thin, steady stream. Stop motor once or twice to scrape down sides of container.

When all of the oil has been incorporated, pour mayonnaise into a small bowl, cover with plastic wrap, and chill thoroughly.

Puree strawberries.

Immediately before serving, stir strawberries into mayonnaise.

Ideas for Using Strawberry Butter

- Use on homemade breads, rolls, muffins, biscuits, pancakes, waffles, or brioches.
- Spread on chicken or fish while grilling or broiling.
- Dot on fruits, such as peaches and apples, before baking.
- Use as a spread for tea sandwiches and canapés; for example, spread on bread or crackers and top with smoked salmon.

Strawberry Butter

makes about ¾ cup

½ cup sliced strawberries
1 tablespoon honey
½ cup butter, cut into small bits, room temperature, divided

In a medium-size bowl, mash together strawberries and honey, using a fork or potato masher. With an electric mixer, gradually beat in half of the butter at medium speed. At first, mixture will not seem to be blending together but it will pull together. After half of the butter has been added, increase speed to high and whip in remaining butter, continuing to beat until mixture is light and fluffy. Pack butter into a small crock or mold and cover tightly with plastic wrap.

Butter will keep for a few days in the refrigerator. It also freezes well.

Variations:

Add cinnamon, nutmeg, mace, ginger, basil, thyme, or chives.

Add ground nuts.

Add finely grated orange, lime, or lemon peel.

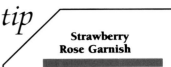

Strawberry Rose Garnish

Thinly slice strawberries lengthwise and arrange the slices in petals (pointed edge out) in a circular, slightly overlapping pattern. Use to top cakes or as a base for salads or ice cream.

Strawberry Dessert Sauce

makes about 2 cups

Enhance ice cream, cakes, or fresh fruit with the addition of this sauce.

1 cup whole strawberries
⅓ cup apple juice
1 cup sliced strawberries
½ cup plain yogurt

Puree whole strawberries with apple juice in a food processor or blender. Stir in sliced strawberries and gently fold in yogurt.

Strawberry Specials

Serve strawberries on skewers with cooked chicken or fish chunks, or toss with one of the following:

- balsamic vinegar
- ground cinnamon
- freshly ground tellicherry peppercorns
- lime or orange juice and rind
- crème fraîche
- vanilla yogurt
- orange juice with a drop of orange-flower water
- Grand Marnier
- cream

Strawberry-Orange Tarts

makes 12 3-inch tarts

Pastry:
  ⅓ cup butter
  ¾ cup whole wheat pastry flour
  1 cup unbleached white flour
  1 teaspoon lemon juice
  5 or 6 tablespoons ice water

Orange Custard:
  3 tablespoons honey
1¼ cups milk, divided
  2 tablespoons cornstarch
  1 egg, beaten
  ½ cup orange juice
  ¼ teaspoon orange extract
  2 cups strawberries, sliced

To prepare the pastry: In a medium-size mixing bowl, cut butter into combined whole wheat flour and white flour with a pastry cutter until it forms into crumbs the size of small peas. Sprinkle lemon juice over mixture. Add ice water, 1 tablespoon at a time, and stir with a fork until dough holds together. Form a ball and wrap with plastic wrap. Refrigerate for 2 hours, or overnight.

When ready to roll, place dough between 2 pieces of plastic wrap or waxed paper. Roll out to a ⅛- to ¼-inch thickness. Cut 12 4-inch circles, rerolling dough only if necessary. Press dough into 3-inch tartlet pans and bake at 425°F for about 12 minutes. Cool and remove from pans.

To prepare the orange custard: In the top of a double boiler, mix honey and ¾ cup of the milk together. Whisk the remaining milk and cornstarch together in a small cup. Whisk into honey mixture. Set over simmering water and heat mixture over medium-low heat, stirring constantly, until slightly thickened. Pour a small amount of the hot mixture into beaten egg, stirring constantly. Pour egg mixture into heated milk mixture and cook for another 5 to 10 minutes over medium-low heat until custard coats the back of a spoon. Remove from heat. Cover with waxed paper and cool to lukewarm. Stir in orange juice and extract. Cover and chill thoroughly.

When ready to assemble, spoon orange custard into tart shells and top with sliced strawberries.

Strawberry Shortbread Pizza

16 servings

Dough:
⅓ cup butter, softened
½ cup honey
 1 egg, beaten
¼ cup milk
¼ teaspoon vanilla extract
¾ cup whole wheat pastry flour
 1 cup unbleached white flour
 1 teaspoon baking powder

Topping:
 8 ounces cream cheese, softened
¼ cup honey
 1 teaspoon vanilla extract
 1 quart strawberries, sliced

To prepare the dough: Beat butter and honey together. Add egg, milk, and vanilla. Sift flours with baking powder. Blend into butter mixture. Cover dough and refrigerate for 1 hour.

Preheat oven to 375°F. Spray a 14-inch-round pizza pan with vegetable spray.

Spread dough into pan. Bake for about 15 minutes, or until golden brown. Cool.

To prepare the topping: Beat together cream cheese, honey, and vanilla. Spread on cooled crust. Arrange sliced strawberries decoratively over top, overlapping slices.

Individually Quick-Frozen Strawberries

Quick freezing is a great way to preserve strawberries. Simply hull and set them on a baking sheet, and place in the freezer. When frozen, transfer the berries to freezer bags or containers and, when you're ready, remove the exact amount you need. Use them without defrosting in pies, tarts, and pastries; in rice pudding; in sauces; in fruit compotes and stewed fruit; over cakes and ice cream; pureed with milk for a refreshing beverage; and in omelets and crepes.

Strawberry puree can also be frozen and defrosted overnight in the refrigerator. Swirl it into vanilla milkshakes and vanilla yogurt, spoon it over fresh fruit, or add buttermilk to it to make a chilled soup.

Index

Rodale Press, Inc., publishes RODALE'S ORGANIC GARDENING®,
the all-time favorite gardening magazine.
For information on how to order your subscription,
write to RODALE'S ORGANIC GARDENING ᴿ, Emmaus, PA 18049.